The Other

Hela

gan / by Mari Izzard

C000130142

CAST:

Erin: Lowri Izzard
Hugh: Gwydion Rhys
The Algorithm: Rhian Blythe

CREADIGOL / CREATIVES:

Dramodydd / Writer: Mari Izzard
Cyfarwyddwr / Director: Dan Jones
Cynllunydd / Designer: Delyth Evans
Cynllunydd Goleuo / Lighting Designer: Katy Morison
Cynllunydd Sain/Cyfansoddwr // Sound Designer/Composer: Tic Ashfield
Fideograffydd / Video Designer: Simon Clode
Rheolwr y Cynhyrchiad / Production Manager: Rhys Williams
Rheolwr Llwyfan / Stage Manager: Theodore Hung
Cyfarwyddwr Ymladd / Fight Director: Kev McCurdy
Cyfarwyddwr Cyswllt / Associate Director: Matthew Holmquist
Cyfarwyddwr Cynorthwyol / Assistant Director: Alice Eklund
Cyfarwyddwr Castio / Casting Director: Nicola Reynolds
Dehonglydd Iaith Arwyddion Prydain (BSL) / BSL Interpreter: Cathryn McShane
Golygydd Sgript / Script Editor: Sioned Ffion
Adeiladwr y Set / Set Builder: Will Goad
Ffotograffydd y cynhyrchiad / Production Photographer: Kirsten McTernan

FRONT COVER IMAGE:

Photography: Simon Clode
Design: Limegreentangerine

Mae *Hela* yn gynhyrchiad gan The Other Room mewn cydweithrediad â Theatr Genedlaethol Cymru/*Hela* is produced by The Other Room in association with Theatr Genedlaethol Cymru.

Hela was first performed at The Other Room, Cardiff from 05/11/2019 – 24/11/2019. It was commissioned and produced as a part of The Violence Series.

The⊃therRoom
at Porter's

Artistic Director & CEO: Dan Jones
Producer: George Soave
Associate Director: Matthew Holmquist
Trainee Director: Nerida Bradley
Trainee Producer: Ben Clark
Press & Marketing Associate: Alys Hewitt
Executive Producers: Dan Porter & David Wilson

The Other Room at Porter's is Cardiff's pub theatre. It was founded by Artistic Director Kate Wasserberg and Executive Director Bizzy Day in response to the exciting opportunity to develop an audience for drama in the heart of Cardiff. An intense, purpose-built space with 47 seats, The Other Room produces great modern plays and new work by and with Welsh, Wales-based and Wales-trained artists. The Other Room has fast established a reputation for quality and daring drama, won Fringe Theatre of the Year at the 2016, Stage Awards, and a plethora of accolades at The Wales Theatre Awards in 2015, 2016 and 2017. The theatre was shortlisted in the Arts category of the Cardiff Life Awards 2017 and 2018, as well as for the prestigious Peter Brook Empty Space Award, 2017. The Other Room is currently run by Artistic Director and CEO, Dan Jones.

The Other Room would like to thank Andrea Hodges, Andrew Havers, Arad Goch, Arts Council England, Arts Council of Wales, Arwel Gruffydd, Cardiff and Vale College, The Carne Trust, Cathy Boyce, Chapter Arts Centre, Claire Bottomley, Corey Bullock, David Bond, Emily Pearce, Emma Evans, The Esmee Fairbairn Foundation, The Garfield Weston Foundation, Hayley Burns, Heather Davies, Julia Barry, The Leche Trust, Matthew Bulgo, Michael Carklin, National Theatre Wales, Philip Carne, Pontio Arts and Innovation Centre, Porter's, Rhian Davies, Royal Welsh College of Music and Drama, Sarah Bickerton, Sherman Theatre, South Wales Police, Theatr Clwyd, Theatrau Sir Gâr, Theatre503, Theatr Genedlaethol Cymru, University of South Wales, Violet Burns, Wales Millennium Centre and Yasmin Williams.

Hela was made possible by the incredible work of founding Executive Director, *Bizzy Day* – whose work as Executive Director, Producer and Fundraiser made this play a reality.

Violet Burns Playwriting Award

This production wouldn't have been possible if it wasn't for the **Violet Burns Playwright Award**. The Award is committed to discovering, nurturing and producing Wales-based, female playwrights and is a steadfast commitment to bringing to the fore unheard voices from across Wales, championing women in theatre to achieve their creative potential.

The Award has been made possible through the generous support of Violet's daughter Hayley, who has created it in memory of her mother.

Violet Burns was born into a working-class family in 1946. Raised in a two-bedroom council house in a small fishing village on the east coast of Scotland, there were insufficient finances available to support the family and she had to leave school early to take up a job in the local Spar. Given her background and the limited opportunities she had been given, she never believed herself capable nor creative, and yet was a secret writer and poet. She never returned to her education despite having a keen interest in both medicine and writing. Violet sadly passed away on 10 January 2017 following a battle with lung cancer.

The Award has been run in association with **Theatr Genedlaethol Cymru**. The Other Room would like to thank Hayley and the Violet Burns Playwriting Award for enabling a challenging and dynamic production from a brilliant playwright.

Nodyn / Note

Roeddwn i eisiau cynnwys nodyn i atgoffa chi – darllenwr, fedrwch chi neud unrhywbeth rydych chi ishe, gan cynnwys ysgrifennu ddrama i lwyfan.

Mae pob gair yn y llyfr bach yma, yn gynnyrch o ddal-ati, lwc, a faint mor hael mae pobol wedi bod efo'i amser a'i caredigrwydd.

Roedd yr 'ods' wedi eu pentyrru'n fy erbyn i, i byth ysgrifennu drama – heb sôn am cael e ei chyhoeddi.

Menyw. Dosbarth gweithiol. Cweer. Cymraeg ond ddim yn digon Cymreig i rhai. Hynod o fucking dyslecsig. Fedrai mynd ymlaen…

Ond os gallai wneud, gall unrhyw un.

*Felly beth ydych chi'n aros am?! Os ydych chi'n grac, yn union fel roeddwn i, codwch blydi pen, a wnewch rywbeth amdano'r peth a **plis** YSGRIFENNWCH!*

Mae'r byd yn aros i glywed eich straeon hefyd.

I wanted to include a note to remind you – dear reader, that if you so wish you can do anything your heart desires, including write a play.

Every word you read in this little book, is a product of stick-with-it-ness, luck and how generous others have been with their time and kindness.

The odds were stacked against me to ever write a play – let alone get it published.

Woman Working class. Queer. Welsh but not Welsh enough for some. Dyslexic as fuck. I could go on..

But if I can do it, anybody can.

So what are you waiting for?! If you're angry, just like I was, pick up a god damn pen, do something about it and **please** WRITE!

The world is waiting to hear your stories too.

DRAMODYDD/WRITER: Mari Izzard

Mari grew up in Bridgend, South Wales and trained as an actor at the Royal Welsh College of Music and Drama, where she first started her writing journey as part of the training on the course. As an actor she has worked for for the Royal Shakespeare Company, Regent's Park Open Air Theatre, National Theatre of Wales and most recently in *Lord of the Flies* for Sherman Theatre and Theatr Clwyd.

Mari was one of Theatr Clwyd and Paines Plough's Writers in Residency as part of their TYFU/GROW scheme in 2017. Other writing credits include: *HRH Prince of Wales 70th Birthday Celebration: The Goons Show Adaptation* for Royal Welsh College of Music & Drama (Dir: Bruce Gutherie) and *Grand* for Split Milk Theatre (Dir. Tamara Williams).

Mari is thrilled to be the inaugural winner of the Violet Burns Playwriting Award.

CAST:

Erin: Lowri Izzard

Lowri graduated from RADA in 2016.

Theatre credits include: *Lord of the Flies* (Sherman Theatre/Theatre Clwyd); *Votes For Women* (New Vic Theatre); *A Midsummer Night's Dream* (Wilton's Music Hall); I *Capture The Castle The Musical* (Watford Palace/Oxford Playhouse); *The Tempest* (The Orange Tree Theatre) and *Much Ado About Nothing* (Faction Theatre).

She also appears as PC Mari James in series 1 & 2 of *Hidden/Craith* for BBC & S4C.

Workshop credits include: *The Boy In The Dress* (The RSC); *Saint George and the Dragon* (National Theatre); *Maid of Orleans* (The Bunker Theatre).

For The Other Room: *American Nightmare.*

Hugh: Gwydion Rhys

TV credits include:
Hinterland (BBC); *Hidden* (BBC); *35 Diwrnod* (S4C); *Parch* (Boom); *Cara Fi* (Touchpaper TV); *Tir* (Joio TV).

Stage credits include:
To Kill a Machine (Scriptography Productions); *Only The Brave* (Soho Theatre / WMC); *The Village Social* (NTW); *Crazy Gary's Mobile Disco / Pornography* (Waking Exploits); *Little Wolf* (Lucid Theatre); *The Wood / One Man Two Guvnors* (Torch Theatre); *Three Nights Blitz* (Swansea Grand Theatre).

For The Other Room: *American Nightmare.*

Llais yr Algorithm/Voice of the Algorithm: Rhian Blythe

Rhian is a Bafta Cymru winner for Best Actress for her work on Gwaith Cartref. She also won Best Actress at the Edinburgh Festival in 2008 for her performance in the multi-award-winning production *Deep Cut.*

Rhian trained at QMUC in Edinburgh, then joined Theatr Genedlaethol Cymru as a core member of the cast for two years. Rhian has worked vastly in theatre, television and radio in Wales and further afield. Including 59 E 59 in New York, The Tricycle and Soho Theatre in London and the Traverse Theatre, Edinburgh.

Rhian's recent credits include: *Keeping Faith* (Vox Pictures); *Hinterland* (Fiction Factory); *Deian a Loli* (Cwmni Da, S4C) and the lead in *Morfydd*, a biopic film for Boom. Rhian is a fluent Welsh speaker.

CREATIVES:

Cyfarwyddwr / Director: Dan Jones

Dan is the current Artistic Director of The Other Room, where he previously worked as both Associate Director and Trainee Director.

Director credits include: *The Awkward Years, The Effect, All But Gone, Constellation Street* (The Other Room); *Blink* (Critical Ambition, The Other Room & Volcano Theatre); *The Man, Romeo And Juliet, Julius Caesar, Song From A Forgotten City* (Critical Ambition).

Associate and Assistant Director credits include: *St Nicholas, The Dying Of Today* (The Other Room); *Alix In Wundergarten* (difficult|stage & The Other Room); *All My Sons* (Theatre Clwyd); *King Of The Sky* (Pontardawe Arts Centre).

Dan has also worked on various rehearsed readings and scratch nights across South Wales, with companies such as Dirty Protest, Sherman Theatre, The Other Room and Critical Ambition.

Dan graduated from the University of Exeter with college commendation and is also Co-Artistic Director of Critical Ambition, Swansea.

Cynllunydd / Designer: Delyth Evans

Delyth trained at The Royal Welsh College of Music and Drama, graduating in 2018. Recent credits include: *American Nightmare*, *The Story* (The Other Room); *How We Begin* (King's Head Theatre); *One Giant Leap* (Brockley Jack); *In Lipstick* (The Pleasance Theatre); *Out of Love* (LAMDA); *All That* (The Kings Head) and *Punk Rock* (RWCMD).

Cynllunydd Goleuo / Lighting Designer: Katy Morison

Katy is a Lighting Designer based in South Wales. She has recently worked on *American Nightmare* by Matthew Bulgo and *The Story* by Tess Berry-Hart, the two plays in The Violence Season at Cardiff's The Other Room; as well as *Shooting Rabbits/Saethu Cwningod* by Powderhouse and *Woof* at Sherman Theatre. Her work in 2018 included *Exodus* for Wales-based company Motherlode and follows from the success of *The Good Earth*, which received 5-star reviews and enjoyed an off-Broadway run in New York to critical acclaim. She also designed three shows as part of National Theatre Wales' NHS70 season.

She has worked as an associate and Re-lighter, as well as Lighting Designer for Venue 13 at the Edinburgh Fringe, and also as a Production Supervisor and lighting tutor at Royal Welsh College of Music and Drama. She was a member of the Production Team at Sherman Cymru for over 7 years.

Cynllunydd Sain/Cyfansoddwr // Sound Designer/Composer: Tic Ashfield

Tic Ashfield (RWCMD) is a BAFTA Cymru Award-Winning Composer and Sound Designer based in South Wales. She has created music and sound for numerous projects including work for film, TV, theatre, dance, animation, installation and educational outreach projects. Commissioners and collaborators include BBC 1 Wales, BBC 2, BBC 4, S4C, All3Media, Fiction Factory, Severn Screen, John Hardy Music, Creative Assembly, National Theatre Wales, The Other Room

Theatre, Taking Flight Theatre, Chippy Lane Productions, Omidaze Productions, Winding Snake Productions, Welsh National Opera, Lighthouse Theatre, Joio and Gwyn Emberton Dance.

As a composer and sound designer she focuses on using a combination of found sound manipulation and sampling, synthesis and instrumental writing to create bespoke soundworlds, often within collaborative settings.

Fideograffydd / Video Designer: Simon Clode

Simon is an artist/ filmmaker whose work intercuts many disciplines, with interests lying in ethnographic, environmental and global political commentary. His films have screened in competition at BAFTA qualifying festivals such as Aesthetica Short Film Festival. He has been a video designer on numerous projects for national and international theatre and dance, as well as working on large scale site specific work like *The Tide Whisperer* and *Now the Hero*. Arts Council Wales supports his artist films with his most recent film installation showing at Palestine's contemporary Arts Festival 'Qalandiya International'. He is currently one of the directors selected for the BFI Network / BAFTA GURU 2019/2020 program, as well as being a BFI Horizons recipient.

Rheolwr y Cynhyrchiad / Production Manager: Rhys Williams

Rhys worked in the Audio Visual industry for over 25 years with responsibilities in deploying worldwide systems and solutions to many corporate giants. In 2018 Rhys decided to change career to follow his passion in the Theatre and Live Events. Since making that decision, Rhys has undertaken a Master's Degree at the Royal Welsh College of Music and Drama in Stage and Event Management. Rhys has worked on many Theatrical and Live Events, most recently Simon Stephens *Rage* and Matthew Bulgo's *American Nightmare*. From technical deployment to process administration, Rhys brings a multitude of skill sets to his Production Management.

Rheolwr Llwyfan / Stage Manager: Theodore Hung

Theodore graduated from the Royal Welsh College of Music and Drama with a Stage Management and Technical Theatre degree in 2017. Apart from pursuing his passion for writing in his spare time, since graduating he has been working extensively in the theatre scene in Cardiff, London and Edinburgh. His previous stage management credits include: ASM for *Highway One* as part of Cardiff's Festival of Voice, SM for *The Chimes* (St.John's Canton/Waterloo); *Tilda Swinton Answer An Ad on Craigslist* (Vault Festival London/Edinburgh Fringe 2019); *Les Miserables* (Chapter Arts Centre) and *Robinson: The Other Island* (Chapter Arts Centre).

Cyfarwyddwr Ymladd / Fight Director: Kev McCurdy

Kev is an Equity professional Fight Director. He primarily trained as an actor at The Royal Welsh College of Music and Drama from 1991 – 1998. He gained his Equity Professional Fight Directors status in 1996. Kev has been Royal Welsh Colleges' resident fight tutor since 2005 and has worked on a variety of stage, TV and film projects around the UK and abroad. Kev was also very honoured to have been awarded The Paddy Crean Fight Award at the event 4 years ago. He was also awarded the RWCMD Fellowship award 2 years ago. He's also the Co-Founder and Chairman for The Academy of Performance Combat. Kev has worked on numerous plays, TV shows, operas, video games and feature films. Some companies he has worked for: Walt Disney, Pixar, Atlas Entertainment, RSC, National Theatre, Old Vic, Young Vic, Shakespeare's Globe, Curve Theatre, Manchester Royal Exchange, BBC, Sky 1, ITV, Channel 4, S4C Wales, Sega.

Cyfarwyddwr Cyswllt / Associate Director: Matthew Holmquist

Matthew is the current Associate Director at The Other Room Theatre as well as Artistic Director of Red Oak Theatre.

Directing credits include: *Cardiff Boy* (Red Oak Theatre, The Other Room); *A Recipe for Sloe Gin* (Clocktower Theatre,

World of Boats); *Blue Stockings* (Sherman Players, Sherman Theatre); *The River* (Red Oak Theatre, Loco Bristol); *We Had a Black Dog* (Red Oak Theatre, Theatre De Menilmontant, Paris).

Associate Director/Staff Director credits include: *Eugene Onegin* (Buxton Opera) *Le Vin Herbe, Don Giovanni* (Welsh National Opera / Opera Cenedlaethol Cymru); *A Christmas Carol* (Simply Theatre, Geneva).

Assistant Director credits include: *Tremor, Taming of The Shrew* (Sherman Theatre) *Simplicius Simplicissimus* (Independent Opera); *Insignificance* (Theatre Clwyd); *Kommilitonen!* (Welsh National Youth Opera / Opera Ieuenctid Cenedlaethol Cymru).

Cyfarwyddwr Cynorthwyol / Assistant Director: Alice Eklund

Alice is an emerging Theatre Director based in Cardiff. Alice studied Film and Television Studies (Welsh medium) at Aberystwyth University. This year Alice's production of *Constellations* by Nick Payne represented Wales as their national champion at the British One Acts Festival at Harrogate Theatre, Harrogate. During this festival the production picked up multiple awards including 'Best Performance' and 'Best Director'. Alice is currently developing a company that will celebrate the womxn that currently create and inspire in Wales.

Credits include: *The Awkward Years*, Matthew Bulgo (Assistant Director, The Other Room); *On Scarborough Front/The Kaiser and I* (Assistant Director, Lighthouse TC); *The Welsh Harpist*, Bex Betton (Director, USW Showcase); *Constellations*, Nick Payne (Director, Unknown Theatre Company); *The 12 Plays of Christmas*, R&D (Assistant Director and Welsh Dramaturgy, The Other Room); *A Night In The Clink*, Matthew Bulgo, Branwen Davies and Tracy Harris (Asst. Dir. and Stage Manager, Papertrail); *The Talking Shop – Pop Up*, Senedd Cymru (Associate Producer, Omidaze).

*This text went to print before the end of rehearsals
so may differ from what is seen on stage.*

*Mae'r ddrama i'w pherfformio'n ddwyieithog
// The play is only ever to be performed bilingually*

Mari Izzard

HELA

OBERON BOOKS
LONDON

WWW.OBERONBOOKS.COM

First published in 2019 by Oberon Books Ltd
521 Caledonian Road, London N7 9RH
Tel: +44 (0) 20 7607 3637 / Fax: +44 (0) 20 7607 3629
e-mail: info@oberonbooks.com
www.oberonbooks.com

Copyright © Mari Izzard, 2019

Mari Izzard is hereby identified as author of this play in accordance with
Section 77 of the Copyright, Designs and Patents Act 1988. The author
has asserted her moral rights.

All rights whatsoever in this play are strictly reserved and application
for performance etc. should be made before commencement of rehearsal
to United Agents, 12-26 Lexington St, Soho, London W1F 0LE.
No performance may be given unless a licence has been obtained, and
no alterations may be made in the title or the text of the play without the
author's prior written consent.

You may not copy, store, distribute, transmit, reproduce or otherwise
make available this publication (or any part of it) in any form, or
binding or by any means (print, electronic, digital, optical, mechanical,
photocopying, recording or otherwise), without the prior written
permission of the publisher.

A catalogue record for this book is available from the British Library.

PB ISBN: 9781786829238
E ISBN: 9781786829221

Printed and bound by 4EDGE Limited, Hockley, Essex, UK.

Visit www.oberonbooks.com to read more about all our books and to buy them. You will
also find features, author interviews and news of any author events, and you can sign up
for e-newsletters and be the first to hear about our new releases.

Printed on FSC® accredited paper

10 9 8 7 6 5 4 3 2 1

Cymeriadau
/
Characters

ERIN

Mam. Menyw browd Gymreig, ffyrnig o benderfynol,
anhygoel o glyfar, merch ffarmwr.

/

A mother. Fiercely determined, proud Welsh woman,
incredibly smart, farmer's daughter.

HUGH

Canol ugeiniau hwyr / tridegau cynnar.
Mab y Prif Weinidog. Swyngyfareddol a uchelgeisiol.

/

Mid-late twenties/Early thirties. Son of the First Minister.
Charming, ambitious.

Gyda phob adran newydd mae amser wedi mynd heibio.
/ With each new section, time has passed.

Gyda diolch o galon i...
The Violet Burns Award, The Other Room, Hayley Burns,
Lowri, Dan, Matthew, Sioned a Mam

Actor – Hogn –
di Gjmraeg?

Oedd
Mari'n
actio yn
y dorama?

Un

Cerddoriaeth yn chwarae - mae'n glitchy ond rydyn ni'n gweld ar yr AV:

MENYW: Diolch

Ond

10%

10%

10%

o debygolrwydd

Felly

anfod/

ON THE AV: algorithm – "algərɪð(ə)m"
"a process / broses
or set of rules / neu set o reolau
to be followed in calculations or other
problem-solving operations, /
i'w ddilyn mewn cyfrifiadau neu
weithrediadau datrys problemau eraill,
especially by a computer./
yn enwedig gan gyfrifiadur."

LLAIS: Croeso i Wlad X. Dywedwyd wrthym y byddwch yn ymweld â'n gwlad am X diwrnod. Rydym yn eich hatgoffa y bydd cosb os fyddwch yn ymestyn eich arhosiad heb ganiatâd.

Glitches. SNAP MUSIC OFF A BLACKOUT.

Rydyn ni nawr mewn lladd-dŷ. Mae popeth y tu mewn i'r ladd-dŷ o ddegawd gwahanol, fel petai eu bod nhw'n hand-me-downs. Mae pethau wedi llusgo ar draws y llawr, "mind maps" wedi eu dinistrio ar y waliau fel petai rhyw ffrae wedi bod.

Rydyn ni'n sylwi bod HUGH, sy'n anymwybodol, gyda gwaed ar ei dalcen, wedi clymu i gadair yng nghanol y llwyfan.

Snap i olau sbot anhygoel o gryf ar HUGH. Mae hyn yn dychryn HUGH.

HUGH: Ah.

That's really –

Shit.

That's bright

1

I can't…

Clywed footsteps.

Daw ERIN i mewn – gwisgo par o dungarees – mae'n dod ar draws yn ifanc iawn

ERIN: Helo?

HUGH: Hello! YES!

I'm over here

Please HELP!

ERIN: Beth sy-?

O madde byw

HUGH: Oh fuck

Quickly!

That light.

It's really hurting my eyes!

Can you turn it off?

Mae ERIN yn sefyll o flaen y golau sbot fel bod ei silhouette hi yn cysgodi llygaid HUGH.

HUGH: That's a little better

But if you could just/

ERIN: Wyt ti'n iawn?

HUGH: I don't know what you're saying

Can you just turn that light off/

ERIN: Wyt ti'n iawn?

HUGH: Jesus

Just turn the light off will you/

ERIN: Beth wyt ti'n neud 'ma?

HUGH yn sylweddoli mae wedi clymu fyny

HUGH: Fuck

    Help

    Please

    Help

    You have to get me out of here

ERIN: Oes 'na rywun sy' eisie dy frifo di neu rywbeth?

HUGH: Is that ugh/

    Are you speaking/

    I'm sorry

    But I don't speak/

ERIN: Pwy 'nath hwn i ti?

HUGH: I – *(Trial symud)*

    I really don't know what you're saying

    So please

    Just help me

    I'm fucking tied up for Christ sake

    Someone's tied me up/

    ERIN yn symud allan o'r golau, i checio'n gloi. HUGH winces.

HUGH: AH Fuck! Please

    That light –

    It's

ERIN: Ie

    Ti 'di cael dy glymu'n

    Eitha' tynn hefyd

    Mae ERIN yn sefyll o flaen y golau sbot eto.

ERIN: Gwell?

HUGH: I guess that's helping

But if you could untie me

That would be so much better

And then I can/

ERIN yn troi'r golau bant ag yn edrych yn agosach.

ERIN: Cyffion ydyn nhw

Oes allwedd?

HUGH: Please

I don't know what you're saying

Or how else to say it

Just untie me will you

UN-TIE M-E

ERIN: Dw i angen allwedd

HUGH: Ugh god

I don't know how else to say it.

ERIN: All-wedd

DW I ANGEN ALLWEDD

HUGH: Is that your name?

I don't know any Ac-wed

ERIN: NA

A-LL-WEDD

"LL"

Fel y sŵn mae cath yn neud

Allwedd

HUGH: Is that your name?

ERIN yn actio allan allwedd.

ERIN: ALLWEDD

HUGH: Oh

4

Key.

Then just say it in Eng/

ERIN yn dal wyneb HUGH.

HUGH: What the/

ERIN: Dy'n nhw ddim yn ffan mawr o'r iaith 'na

Meddwl bod Erin eisiau cusannu Hugh. Yn rhyddhau ei wyneb gyda phat bach a gwên.

M'ond yn trial helpu…
Yn codi ei wallt gyda'i bys.

Fydd rhaid i ni lanhau hwnna.
ERIN yn ffeindio cwpn o beth rydyn ni'n meddwl yw dŵr. ERIN yn cymrud sip.

HUGH: Please

Is that water?

Can I have some/

Mae hi'n dipio'i bys i mewn ac yna'n cyffwrdd clwyf HUGH ar ei dalcen.

HUGH: AH

Jesus

What is that?

ERIN: Vodka

HUGH: Surely you can't be old enough to be drinking that/

ERIN: Ydy e'n boenus?

Rhoi dolur?

HUGH: I'm sorry

But you clearly understand what I'm saying

So why are you still choosing to talk at me in/

ERIN: Ti ddim hyd yn oed yn deall tipyn bach?

HUGH: "Bach"!

Bach is little isn't it?

ERIN: Felly rwyt ti yn deall?

HUGH: "Tipyn bach"

Is that right?

I can't speak it anymore see.

ERIN: Ac erbyn nawr ti 'di anghofio?

Wedi bod yn rhedeg am rhy hir

Wedi ailystyried pwy wyt ti?

Newid dy acen di,

Blah blah blah

R'un math o fullshit

HUGH: All I got from that was blah blah blah, bullshit.

ERIN: Wyt ti eisie deall yn well?

Falle mae 'na ffordd...

Saib.

Wyt ti eisie deall yn well

Hugh?

HUGH: How do you know my name?

ERIN: Wyt ti eisie deall yn well?

HUGH: How the fuck do you know my name?!

ERIN: Dw i'n gofyn cwestiwn i ti

Ac mae'n rhaid i ti ateb

Neu fyddwn nhw'n grac iawn

HUGH: Cwestiwn

Question

Right?

Clap araf.

ERIN: Llongyfs Hedd Wyn

Ti ar dy ffordd i fod yn rhugl.

Wyt ti eisie deall yn well?

HUGH: Whatever it is you're asking –

It feels like you want me to say yes.

ERIN: Ydw.

HUGH: And if I don't –

Because you do realise

I don't know what I'm agreeing to/

ERIN: Gei di wybod os wyt ti eisie

Ond bydd hi lot haws i bawb fan hyn os atebi di

HUGH: I'm not being funny

But

Who even are you?

ERIN: Ges i fy nanfon i dy helpu di

Ond dwyt ti ddim hyd yn oed

Yn deall beth dw i'n dweud

Felly beth yw'r/

HUGH: How old are you?

ERIN: Dyfala!

HUGH: I know you're probably a

Teenager

Maybe

But how many times I have to say this to you

I do not know what you are asking me to agree to

Do you understand that?

ERIN: Wyt ti eisie deall yn well neu beidio?

Wyt ti eisie deall yn well?

Ateb fi.

Wyt ti eisie deall yn well?

Wyt ti eisie deall yn well?/

HUGH: Yes?

ERIN: Ydw

HUGH: Yes.

ERIN: Ydw

HUGH: Yes.

ERIN: Mae'n rhaid i ti ddweud "Ydw".

D'wed "Ydw"

"Ydw"

Saying it slowly.

YD-WW

Saib.

HUGH: "yd-ww"

ERIN: Wnawn ni drial 'to te.

"MYFANWY" cyfiethwch a'r gyfer Hugh

Mae ERIN yn datgelu dyfais sy'n debyg i Alexa ac o hyn mlaen mae is-deitlau yn cyfiethu'r Gymraeg i Saesneg yn fyw.

ERIN: Ydy e'n boenus?

HUGH yn sylweddoli ei fod e'n gallu darllen y cyfieithiad.

HUGH: How is it/

ERIN: Dy ddolur di/

HUGH: Doing that?

ERIN: Ydy e dal yn boenus?

HUGH: Yes.

Stinging.

How have you managed that?

How is it translating like that/

ERIN: Druan. *(Mae hi'n taflu'r vodka yn ei wyneb ar "ddamwain".)*
HUGH: WHAT THE-

FUCK!

AHHHHHHHH

IT'S IN

MY EYES

FUCK.

ERIN: O dw i mor mor flin

Mae'n ddrwg gen i

Sori

Ond o leiaf

Mae'n glanhau dy gwt di/

HUGH yn ceisio ond yn methu sychu'r hylif o'i lygaid.

HUGH: UGH YOU –

FOR FUCK SAKE

I can't wipe my fucking eyes because of these fucking/

ERIN: O wps

Nes i ddim meddwl am hynny

Sori

Sori

Sori

Mae ERIN yn sychu ei wyneb.

ERIN: *(Sibrwd)* Ond ti newydd rhegi o'm mlaen i

A fydden nhw ddim yn lico hwnna

HUGH: What

No

I didn't mean it

It was just because of the vodka in my eyes

Am I a hostage?

ERIN: Na

'Dyw'r gair gwystl ddim yn dy siwtio di.

HUGH: What's that supposed to mean/

ERIN: Pwy wyt ti te?

HUGH: Did they tell you my name?

Or are you like Twelve or Eleven or whatever her name is?

ERIN: Wrth gwrs

Ond dw i ddim yn gofyn be' ydy dy enw di

Dw i'n gofyn

Pwy wyt ti?

Hugh.

Saib.

HUGH: Let's be honest

It's not like it's hard to find out

To be fair

My Dad is

Well

My Dad

After all

ERIN: Ie

Am wn i

HUGH: So they told you?

You know,

For a girl your age

I would have thought you'd have figured it out yourself

ERIN: Defnyddio'r wê ti'n feddwl?

Achos mae pobl oedran fi yn wirion gyda'r wê

Nagyn ni.

Dw i'n cael fy nghadw yma yn union fel ti

HUGH: But you do know who I am

Right?

ERIN: Ydw

D'wedon nhw wrthai

HUGH: You keep saying "they"

Who are they?

And what do they want with me?

ERIN: *(Shrug.)*

Nhw

Dw i ddim yn hollol siwr.

Dw i'n neud fel ma nhw'n dweud wrthai

Neu fydda i fyth yn rhydd

HUGH: Is that how this works?

If I do what they say they'll let me go?

ERIN: Am wn i

HUGH: So there's a chance I can get out?

ERIN: Posib - wedi clywed storiau

Ond dw i'n meddwl naethon nhw ladd y boi diwethaf.

Felly, pwy a ŵyr

HUGH: Fuck

Okay

Okay

How do I get them to let me go?

Or at least untie me?

ERIN: Dw i ddim yn gwybod i ddweud y gwir

HUGH: Fuck

ERIN: Stopio rhegi i ddechrau 'da, siwr o fod

HUGH: How did you get out of your chains?

ERIN: Eistedd yn dawel

HUGH: Okay I can do that

ERIN: Am wythnos

HUGH: Okay no I can't do that

ERIN: Iawn te

Eistedd mewn cyffion am byth bythoedd

Siwtia dy hunan

ERIN yn mynd i adael.

HUGH: NO NO PLEASE

COME BACK

I'll do anything

Please

ERIN: Unrhywbeth?

Pe bai lan i fi

Onest, byddwn i wedi neud yn barod

Ond d'yn nhw ddim yn mynd i fod yn bles iawn

Os fyddwn nhw'n darganfod bod

Carcharor arall wedi dy adael yn rhydd.

Ond faset ti wir yn neud unrhywbeth?

Achos os fydd hi werth fy amser/

HUGH: Yes

Anything

Please

Don't make me beg

ERIN: Iawn.

Wnai aros 'te

HUGH: For me to beg?

ERIN: Na

Wnai aros fan hyn

Wnai dy helpu di

Os wnei di be dw i eisie

HUGH: Okay

Anything you need

Saib.

ERIN: Wna i gyfnewid yr addewid pan dw i'n barod

Ha

Nath hwnna odli

HUGH: So you're a prisoner too?

ERIN: Ydw

HUGH: I didn't think you were/

ERIN: Wel, dw i newydd ddweud wrtho ti

HUGH: No I mean until you just said that

What are you/ *(In for?)*

ERIN: Beth wnaeth wneud ti dybio hynny 'te?

HUGH: Well/

ERIN: Ife achos bo' fi'n iau na ti

Fedrai hi ddim o bosib

Neu achos fy mod i'n ddeniadol/

HUGH: *(Snigger.)* You think a lot of yourself/

ERIN: Pam na ddylwn i ddim feddwl lot o'n hunan?

Ti'n cael meddwl lot o dy hunan

Heb i mi farnu ti/

HUGH: Christ

That's not what I meant

ERIN: Pam na allai i fod yn garcharor te?

HUGH: No no I didn't mean it like/

You can

If you want to

It's just that logistically/

ERIN: Does dim ffordd

Allu di fod yn rhannu cell

Gyda merch

Fy oedran i

HUGH: Well yes…

She picks up a rubix cube that is placed on her desk.

ERIN: Dwi 'di bod yn trial datrys hwn am ddwy flynedd.

A dw i'n credu heno fe wna i ei ddatrys.

HUGH: It's taken you two years to solve a puzzle?

ERIN: Ie

 Pam?

HUGH: It's just –

 I don't really give a shit about your rubix cube

 I need you to help me escape

ERIN: Oeddet ti'n gwybod,

 Ar gyfartaledd mae'n cymryd

 Tua ugain symudiad i gwblhau rubix cube?

 Ma' 'da fi tair symudiad ar ôl, Hugh

HUGH: You aren't even listening to me

 How old even are you?

ERIN: Digon hen i ddeall pam dw i yma

HUGH: What?

ERIN: Ni yma achos ein penderfyniadau Hugh.

 Eu canlyniad nhw.

 Rwyt ti yma,

 Achos dy benderfyniadau ti dy hun.

 HUGH yn speechless.

HUGH: My own decisions?

ERIN: O paid bod fel 'na Hugh

HUGH: I didn't decide to tie myself to a chair

ERIN: Na

 Fi nath dy glymu di

 Ond odd rhaid i fi dy glymu di

 Achos dywedon nhw wrtha i,

 Ac o'n i'n ofni byddet ti'n brifo dy hun

15

A fyddet ti ddim 'di gwrando

Fi'n gwybod bo' ti ddim yn fy nghredu i

D'yw dy wyneb di ddim yn dda yn ei guddio fe

Ond i brofi fe

Gei di wybod ychydig bach amdana i

Fy enw i 'di Erin

Dw i'n ferch i ffarmwr

Dwi ar fy mhen fy hun

'Mond fi

Pobl yn meddwl fy mod i'n wallgof

Ac efalle bo' nhw'n iawn

Dw i'm yn eu beio nhw

Nawr

Chwaraewn ni gêm fach i basio'r amser?

HUGH: Absolutely not

I don't want to play a game

While somebody else

Decides whether I get to live or die

Thank you very much

I need to think of a way out of here

Before they kill me first

ERIN: Wel nagyn ni gyd yn marw yn y pendraw?

HUGH: That's rather fucking hippie dippie of you

Considering I'm tied to a chair

And my chances of being killed

Are significantly higher than yours right now

ERIN: Pam wyt ti yma?

HUGH: I don't know

I just remember being at the petrol station.

ERIN: Na.

Pam wyt ti yma – yma

Yng Ngwlad X

Saib.

Pwy oeddet ti'n ymweld?

HUGH: I came for a funeral/

ERIN: Angladd pwy?

Saib.

ERIN: Angladd pwy?

HUGH: It's none of your business

ERIN: Angladd pwy?

HUGH: I'm finding your prying really quite intrusive

ERIN: Angladd pwy?

HUGH: I don't have to tell you anything

ERIN: Angladd pwy?

Saib.

Os dwyt ti ddim eisie dweud

Ma hwnna'n iawn

Saib.

Ond

Ble mae dy Dad di Hugh?

Saib.

Hugh

Ble mae dy Dad di?

HUGH: It was his funeral.

ERIN: Ac odd dy Dad yn ddyn

Parchus?

Llwyddiannus?

Tad da?

HUGH: What's my dead Dad got to do with this?

ERIN: Ateb y cwestiwn Hugh.

Mae hi'n cerdded tuag ato yn edrych ar ei freichiau.

ERIN: Wow

Mae dy freichiau di'n hynod o flewog

HUGH: Of course they are

I'm a grown fucking man

Mae ERIN yn tynnu rhai o gwallt braich HUGH allan.

HUGH: WHAT THE FUCK

ERIN: WOW

Mae hynny'n lot!

Ti'n mynd i ateb y cwestiwn nawr te Hugh?

O'dd dy Dad yn ddyn gonest?

HUGH: I suppose so

Yes.

ERIN: Odd?

HUGH: Odd.

Mae ERIN gwasgu chwarae ar dyfais cerddoriaeth. Mae'n chwarae'n uchel iawn. Mae angen iddo wneud i'r cynudlleidfa neidio a eisiau orchuddio eu glustiau.

Mae ERIN yn dawnsio iddo - yn ffyrnig. Nid yw hyn yn bert mewn unrhyw ffordd.

Mae HUGH yn ceisio ei orau i sgrechian dros ben y gerddoriaeth, ond mae mor uchel mae'n amhosib ei glywed.

Mae'r golau'n newid ac rydyn ni nawr yn "flashback".
ERIN yn codi'r mapiau meddwl sydd wedi'u gwasgaru ar y
llawr, mae'n cael eu taflunio ar hyd a lled yr AV. Mae hi'n
sylweddoli mae'r person mae wedi bod yn aros am wedi
cyrraedd y sefydliad benodol.

WOMAN: Diolch i chi am gyfrannu Rydym wedi adolygu'ch manylion Dim ond 10% o debygolrwydd Oherwydd tebygolrwydd isel Achos ei brosesu ymhellach. Diolch i chi am eich pryder

DARLLENWR NEWYDDION: Heddiw rydyn ni fel gwlad yn galaru ein cyn arweinydd. Roedd e'n ddyn parchus a theuluol, ac rydym fel cenedl yn mynd i weld eisiau ei arweinyddiaeth yn fawr iawn. Mae'n siwr eich bod chi, y gwylwyr, yn cytuno ein bod ni mewn dyled iddo am ein harwain ni tuag at ein gogoniant. Rydym yn danfon ein dymuniadau gorau at ei fab sy'n mynychu'r angladd ac yn dathlu ei fywyd heddiw.

Mae'r golau'n newid yn ôl ac rydyn ni nawr nôl i'r bresennol.
Mae ERIN yn cadw syllu ar HUGH, gan ddod yn agosach. Pan
mae'n edrych fel ei bod hi ar fin ei gusanu, mae hi'n stopio'r
gerddoriaeth.

DAU

Mae hi'n codi caeadau ei lygaid un ar y tro ac ar fin rhoi
goleuni arnyn nhw, ymgais wael i fod yn feddyg.
ERIN: Mae nhw wedi gofyn i fi

I wirio nad oes gyfergyd 'da ti.

Sawl bys ydw i'n dal i fyny?

HUGH: Five

ERIN: Sawl bys ydw i'n dal fyny?

HUGH: Five

ERIN: Sawl bys ydw i'n dal fyny?

HUGH: Ugh

Pump, right?

ERIN: Na

Pedwar ag un bawd

HUGH: Pedwar ag un bawd

ERIN: Ti'n gweld

Ti'n gallu neud e

Da iawn ti.

Beth yw'r peth olaf ti'n cofio 'te?

HUGH: I was at a petrol station.

ERIN: Roeddet ti yn yr orsaf betrol.

HUGH: I was just putting the pump back down

ERIN: Roeddet ti'n rhoi'r pwmp nôl lawr.

HUGH: When I

Something,

Bwrw –

My head

ERIN: GRÊT

Da iawn ti

Siwr dy fod ti'n iawn

A does dim gyfergyd da ti,

Wel

Eithaf siwr.

Ond

Dw i mor sori Hugh

Achos

Fi wnaeth dy fwrw di

Ar dy ben

Dw i'n gwybod

Menyw

ifanc

Fach

Fel fi

Yn pwno ti

Sioc

Arswyd!

Ond ges i orchymyn

Cwmpest ti i'r llawr

Wrth ymyl dy gar di.

'Odd y boi tu ôl i'r til yn help mawr i roi ti yn sedd y car

Ddes i â ti yma

A llusgais i ti mewn i fan hyn

Ac ystyried dy faint di

'Odd e'n lot haws i gael ti yn y gadair nag o'n i'n ei feddwl

Ond ti yma nawr.

Saib. HUGH yn syllu ar ERIN.

ERIN yn edrych tu ôl iddi, i wirio.

ERIN: Ar beth wyt ti'n edrych?

HUGH: You

You

Kidnapped me

ERIN: Dw i mor sori

Ond

Do

HUGH: Why –

    Why me/

ERIN: 'Odd dim dewis gyda fi

    'Odd rhaid i fi

HUGH: I guess it

    Explains why my head is pounding

    And how I got this –

    Ar pen fi.

    You

    Really

    Hit

    Me?

ERIN: Yn union.

    Ond dw i'n mynd i dy helpu di

    Addo

HUGH: Untie me then!

ERIN: Dw i methu neud hynny

    (Dim eto)

    Mae'n rhaid i ti chwarae

    Ennill dy ffordd allan

    Dyna'r unig ffordd

    ERIN yn codi'r rubix cube, yn feddwl drosti.

ERIN: Ti erioed wedi gorffen rubix ciwb o'r blaen?

HUGH: Na

    I don't think so

ERIN: Na, ti ddim yn edrych fel allet ti chwaith.

HUGH: Why/

ERIN: Ti'n edrych yn rhy-

Ti ddim yn ymddangos fel y math o berson.

HUGH: What's that supposed to mean?!

Give us a go and I'll show you that I can

But

You'll have to untie –

Ugh

Bydd –

Bydd rhaid i ti/

ERIN: Di-gyffio?

Datgloi?

Datglymu?

HUGH: Why does it do that?

Make a simple word sound really complicated.

I don't know why you all still care so much

For a language that's completely irrelevant to the rest of us

I think it's actually really rude

ERIN: 'Drycha Hugh

Dw i ddim yn mynd i

ddi-gyffio

ddatglymu

neu eu

datgloi

nhw i ti,

tan fydd y foment iawn yn cyflwyno'i hun

A falle hyd yn oed pryd hynny-

Ond ddim eto iawn?

Dw i angen i ti ateb cwpwl o gwestiynau yn gyntaf.

A naill ai allet ti ei wneud e

Y ffordd hawdd,

Cydweithiol,

Neu

Fyddan nhw'n neud e'n galetach i ti

I neud yn siwr,

I gael yr atebion pa bynnag ffordd

Artaith

HUGH yn chwerthin – disbelief.

ERIN: Sai'n gelwyddgi.

HUGH yn chwerthin mwy

ERIN: Paid chwerthin

Dw i'n gwbwl ddifrifol!

HUGH: Jesus Christ

Oh whoops

Sorry sorry

Iesu Christ

This is just –

Well-a jiw-jiw

It's just that well

POPTY-FUCKING-PING

This is so ridiculous

I can't believe

That a little girl

Has tied me up

And

And is threatening me with torture

I can't take you seriously

AT ALL

ERIN: *(Kickio yn ei groin.)* DOES NEB YN GWEUD POPTYPING

HUGH: FUCK

AH

ERIN: Ti'n meddwl bo' fi'n gelwyddog?

HUGH: I don't/

What's gelwee-ddog?

ERIN: Darllena'r cyfieithiad

HUGH: Can't –

Methu really edrych fyny right now…

ERIN: Os yw celwyddgi yn "liar"

Celwyddog yw…

Os wyt ti'n

Gelwyddgi

Celwyddgi yw'r enw ar gyfer rhywun sy'n dweud celwyddau.

Celwyddog yw'r ferf

Sef –

HUGH: Lying.

ERIN: Dal 'mlan yn gyflym on'd wyt?

Pa ffordd wyt ti'n dewis te Hugh?

ERIN yn mynd i'w gicio eto ond yn stopio.

HUGH: I'll answer!

I swear

I'll do anything

Please.

Just

Don't –

brifo fi.

ERIN: Bach yn hwyr am hynny.

HUGH: No please don't/

ERIN yn prodio y clwyf ar ben ei dalcen ag ac yn ei ddal.
HUGH winces.
Cerddoriaeth. Goleuadau'n newid ac yn mynd â ni at
"flashback".
Sgrin AV yn ymddangos fenyw, mae ERIN yn gwylio'r sgrin yn
ofalus.

WOMAN: Diolch i chi am gyfrannu eich achos i'r system
gyfiawnder droseddol.

Rydym wedi adolygu manylion eich achos a gyda
chymorth ein system algorhythmau, penderfynwyd mai
dim ond 10% o debygolrwydd ddigwyddodd yr achos a
reportiwyd.

Oherwydd isafswm y tebygolrwydd fe ddigwyddodd y
drosedd yma, mae'n annhebygol iawn y caiff eich achos ei
brosesu ymhellach.

Diolch i chi am eich pryder ac am gymryd yr amser i
gadw'ch gwlad yn ddiogel.

ERIN yn torri.

WOMAN: Diolch Diolch Diolch

Diolch i chi am gyfrannu eich achos

Wedi adolygu

manylion

manylion

pen pen

penderfynwyd mai dim ond

10% 10%

10%

10%

10%

o debygolrwydd

Oherwydd isafswm y tebygolrwydd

Mae'n annhebygol iawn y caiff eich achos ei brosesu

ymhellach. Mae'n annhebygol

Mae'n annhebygol

iawn iawn iawn

caiff eich achos ei brosesu ymhellach

Mae'n annhebygol iawn

Mae'n annhebygol

annhebygol

Dilyniant symud byr iawn sy'n cael ei lenwi gyda'r ddeialog

ganlynol:

Lleisiau: COFIWCH: MAE'R RHIENI AR FAI

HASHTAG SPOILER, HI NATH LADD E

GWAHARDD

ALLTUDIAETH

LLOFRUDDIWR

ERIN: Annhebygol

TRI

Nôl i'r diwrnod presennol. Fel breuddwyd, mae ERIN yn torri allan o'r foment sy'n ei phoeni. Mae'n dechrau glawio, ERIN cymryd e i fewn.

ERIN: Dw i'n caru'r glaw

'Dyw lot o bobol ddim

Meddwl ei fod e'n anghyfleus

Ond dw i wastad wedi.

Pan o'n i'n cerdded nôl o'r ysgol

O'n i arfer stopio yn y glaw

Tynnu'n 'sgidiau i

A rhedeg drwyddo fe

Achos chi'n gwlychu fwy os ydych chi'n rhedeg.

A dw i ddim yn sôn am ryw

Gawodydd Mis Ebrill

Na

Dw i'n sôn am y fath law fel

Petai'r nefoedd 'di agor

Ac mae'r diferion yn pwno dy groen di

Weithiau yn gadael cleision bach

Felly o'n i'n stopio yn yr un safle bob tro

Reit ar ben y bryn

Ac o'n i'n sefyll ynddo

Yn derbyn y glaw

Jyst i wneud yn siwr

O'n i medru teimlo

'nath e fy ngwlychu drwyddo

O'n i'n lico'r ffordd o'n i'n arogli

persawr y glaw.

Ti'n sychedig Hugh?

HUGH: I still have that vodka taste dal yn ceg fi.

ERIN: Ond wyt ti'n sychedig?

HUGH: Ydw.

Mae hi'n cerdded i'w desg, i dynnu dec o gardiau a panda pop,
mae'n dod o hyd i welltyn iddo ymysg yr annibendod.

ERIN: Dyma sut mae'r gêm yn gweithio Hugh.

Nhw sy'n gofyn y cwestiynau

Ti'n ateb yn gywir

A gei di ddiod.

Ti'n deall?

HUGH nods.

ERIN: Ac os dwyt ti ddim

Wel/

Oh my god.

Dylwn ni neud e fel The Chase.

O

Gwell

Mastermind.

Ie.

Mastermind.

A galla i fod yn Magnus Magnusson.

Enw fel petai odd 'i rhieni e eisie iddo fe gael ei fwlio ond/

HUGH: Ti'n joio this?

ERIN: Ydw.

Fi'n rili lico gemau.

HUGH: So this a gêm i ti?

>Everyone getting a kick

>Out of the fact I'm being held

>A fucking prisoner?

ERIN: Ydw

>I fod yn hollol onest 'da ti.

Mae hi'n shufflo'r cardiau ac yn eu gosod allan yn mewn tair pentwr.

>ERIN: Gei di ddewis pa gerdyn

>*Saib.*

>Ti'n' dwp neu rywbeth?

>Dewisa'r fucking cerdyn!

HUGH: That one

ERIN: C'mon

>Dewisa bentwr!

>Un

>Dau

>Neu

>Dri

HUGH: That one –

>Un

ERIN yn pigo lan cerdyn.

ERIN: Dy enw llawn di yw Hugh Jenkins?

HUGH: Ie.

>*Mae hi'n caniatáu sip o'r panda pop iddo.*

ERIN: Ta-da!

>*Mae nhw'n syllu ar ei gilydd am eiliad.*

>ERIN: Piga eto.

HUGH: Ugh

Dau

ERIN yn pigo lan cerdyn.

ERIN: Gest di dy eni a'th fagu yma?

HUGH: Ie

Mae hi'n caniatáu sip o'r panda pop iddo.

ERIN: Ta-da!

Mae'n ceisio yfed llawer ohono. Mae ERIN yn ei dynnu i ffwrdd pan mae hi'n sylweddoli.

Mae hi'n fflicio ei drwyn, cosb.

ERIN: Paid twyllo!

HUGH: Ah Jesus

My eyes are watering

C'mon!

ERIN: Rhaid i ti haeddu fe

Eto

C'mon mun,

'Dyw e ddim yn galed

HUGH: Tri

ERIN yn pigo lan cerdyn.

ERIN: Ai arweinydd y wlad hon oedd dy dad?

HUGH: Ie.

ERIN: Ta-da

Mae hi'n caniatáu sip o'r panda pop iddo, yn chwarae yn ôl y rheolau.

ERIN: Eto.

HUGH: Dau.

ERIN yn pigo lan cerdyn.

ERIN: Beth am dy fam?

HUGH: What/

ERIN: Dy fam?

HUGH: How do you/

ERIN: Ddysgodd hi'r iaith i ti?

HUGH: I can't

Please/

ERIN: Beth am dy Fam, Hugh?

Saib.

Os nad wyt ti'n ateb fy nghwestiwn i Hugh,

Mae nhw'n mynd i 'neud hyn yn lot waeth i ti

"MYFANWY" beth yw peth olaf archwiliais?

MYF: Bwrdd Dŵr.

Wyt ti eisiau defnyddio

Bwrdd Dŵr?

ERIN: Hugh

Ti'n gwybod beth yw Bwrdd Dŵr –

Na,

Ma' Bwrdd Dŵr yn swnio fel cachu.

Triwch enw arall MYFANWY.

MYF: Clawr Dŵr?

ERIN: Clawr Dŵr?

Achos mae'n gorchuddio dy wyneb di.

Na

Triwch 'to

MYF: Astell Ddŵr?

ERIN: Na

Triwch 'to

MYF: Styllen Ddŵr

ERIN: Ie

Styllen Ddŵr

Ti'n gwybod beth yw Styllen Ddŵr Hugh?

MYFANWY

Rhowch gyfieithiad ar gyfer Hugh

MYF: "Water Boarding"

Neu Styllen Ddŵr,

Yn fath o arteithio

Lle ma' dŵr yn cael ei harllwys dros frethyn

Sy'n gorchuddio'r wyneb a'r darnau anadlu,

Ac mae'n cau'r Ocsigen bant, 'mond digon,

I 'neud i'r person deimlo fel petai yn boddi.

ERIN: Swnio fel rhywbeth licet ti brofi Hugh?

HUGH: Not really, no

ERIN: Ateba'r cwetiwn de

Os gweli di'n dda.

HUGH: I'm not really sure why

But you're very angry for such a little girl

Has anyone ever told you that?

ERIN yn edrych yn ei desg ac yn ddod o hyd i frethyn a case o panda pops.

HUGH: NO NO

Please

COME BACK

I was only joking

It was just a joke

Where are you going?

What are you –

No I didn't mean it

Please –

ERIN yn mynd i arllwys y botel dros frethyn, i'w wlychu.

ERIN: Dw i'n sori Hugh

Ond hwn yw'r drefn

Os nad wyt yn cydweithio/ gyda nhw

HUGH: Please

Don't.

Mae ERIN yn mynd i ddal y brethyn ar wyneb HUGH.

HUGH: Please!!

NO!

I'll tell you

She stops.

Please

Mae ERIN yn tynnu'r brethyn i ffwrdd o wyneb HUGH.

HUGH: I have reason to believe/

I think my mother is dead.

ERIN: Credu?

HUGH: Yes.

I've not seen or heard from-

Well for a long time

And I don't –

I can't really speak the language

Because

It was for spending time with Mum

Our own secret code.

ERIN: Felly?

Sut aeth hi?

Saib.

Mae ERIN yn mynd i roi'r brethyn ar wyneb HUGH.

HUGH: NO

I'll – I'll

Tell you.

Saib.

The last time I saw her,

Her and my father were arguing.

My father always had a temper,

And he battered her –

Well all of us really

But she got the brunt of it, I think.

And one night,

They were rowing

I don't remember what about

I heard her screaming at him,

Proper screaming

Animal

Guttural

Screams.

It got worse somehow,

That bad that even a kid knows it's not right

So I got up out of bed,

And I walked downstairs

I peaked my head through the living room door

I could see her backed in to the corner

I walked in

I remember

Saying

"Mami – beth sy'n bod?"

She said

"Dim byd cariad, cer nôl i'r gwely"

And I remember her face being red and wet

My father then –

Slammed the door in my face.

And,

I

Believed her.

So, I went back to bed.

The next thing

Thud against something solid

Crac

And the screaming stopped

I never –

Saw her again

I tried asking

My father

But I never got anything from him.

Ddistaw

Pob tro

No matter how much I tried,

Dim byd.

So after years,

O gofyn,

Stopias,

Asking.

And I couldn't bring myself to –

Siarad yr iaith.

ERIN: Ond ti'n siarad e nawr gyda fi

HUGH: Ie cos you're making me

ERIN: Neud i ti

HUGH: O whatever!

Gormod o pobol yn rhy fucking precious

So iaith ti'n perfect anyway

If your biggest problem

Is preserving its purity

You need to open your fucking eyes

And roll with the times

ERIN: Heb buryddion

Fel fi

Fel fy nheulu

Bydden ni dal yn gaethweision

Iddyn nhw dros y bont

Ti'n deall 'ny?

Heb eithafwyr

Radicaliaid

Y gwaed a pherfedd

Ar gyfer newid

Bydden ni'n dal i feddwl

Mai dyna'r cyfan o'n ni'n haeddu

Iawn i ti

Dw i'n siwr

Cael rhedeg

Ac anghofio pwy wyt ti –

DER' MLAEN

Piga!

HUGH: Tri

Erin yn pigo cerdyn.

ERIN: 'Nes di fethu ym Mhrifysgol y Gyfraith?

HUGH: How do you…

Does neb yn/

ERIN: Ma' gyda nhw

Ffyrdd o ddarganfod be' ni angen.

HUGH: What do they want efo fi?

Fi'n tied up,

Siarad iaith ti

Chwarae some fucking card game

Ydy nhw eisiau arian?

Os ti'n gadael fi mynd I can get you/

ERIN: 'Dyn nhw ddim eisie arian

Dw i jyst angen i ti ateb fy nghwestiynau.

Dewisa bentwr.

HUGH: Un

Erin yn pigo cerdyn.

ERIN: Oes gen ti unrhyw frodyr neu chwiorydd?

HUGH: Na

    Dau

Erin yn pigo cerdyn.

ERIN: Pam wyt ti ddim yn byw yma bellach?

HUGH: I got

    Anfon i ffwrdd

    Ar ôl ysgol

    Roedd Dad fi

    Wanted me to go and learn about myself.

ERIN: A 'nest di?

HUGH: I suppose I did

    Ie

ERIN: Be' ddysgest di te?

    Saib.

    Be' ddysgest di?

HUGH: Dim yn gwybod

    I can't really think right now

ERIN: Be' ddysgest di?

HUGH: Methu realli cofio

    I'm a bit tied up.

ERIN: Be' ddysgest di?

HUGH: Why do you care?

    No, seriously

    Why do you want to know?

    It's not like –

    I don't gweld

Any sort of microphone or –

Neu clywed

For that matter

Unrhyw fath o feed

Telling you what to ask

ERIN: Be' ti'n feddwl?

HUGH: You haven't even –

Gadael this room unwaith

Ti ddim hyd yn oed wedi cael any sort of call

ERIN: Na

Ond ges i alwad

Oddi wrth Dduw

HUGH: There's –

There's not even anything written on those cards

Oh for fuck sake

Fuck

HUGH yn chwerthin.

It's –

TI

Isn't it?!

ALL OF THIS?!

ERIN: Ah shit

Dyfalu da!

HUGH: WYT TI'N FUCKING SERIOUS

How could I be so fucking stupid

None of this is real

There isn't a "they" is there?

Ti just yn fucking psycho little bitch

Mae gyd yn ti

isn't it?

ISN'T IT?

UNTIE ME

NAWR

OR I SWEAR/

ERIN: Mae'n ddrwg gen i

Ond dw i ddim yn gallu neud hynny

HUGH: Pam?!

ERIN: Achos rwyt ti bach yn grac ar hyn o bryd

HUGH: Because you're holding me as a fucking prisoner!

Or are you enjoying using me

Like a puppet or something?

Am I bait?

For rhywbeth

Or rhywun arall?

You dragged me back to

Beth?

Your little Wendy house?

Your bunker?

You think this is all some sort of game?

I'm so confused

I just want to go home

Please

Let me go home

I have a family

And they need me

Please

Dwi ddim

I don't

PAM

I don't deserve this

I bet

Ye

I bet you're just some sick

Stalker

Domineering bitch

That gets off from cuffing people up.

ERIN: Byddai hynny'n hwyl dw i'n siwr.

Ond na.

Nid fy arddull i 'di hwnna.

HUGH: Then why am I –

Why me?

ERIN: Achos dw i 'di bod yn aros

Amdanat ti.

Ife 'na be' ti eisie clywed?

HUGH: You've been waiting/

ERIN: Ydw

Aros amdanat ti

'Na beth 'wedes i.

Cerdyn arall te.

Saib. ERIN yn cydio yn "meat hook" sy'n hongian o'r nenfwd, yn edrych arno, yn dal y pen miniog ac yn ei daro HUGH efo'r handlen ar ei asgwrn doniol.

HUGH: AH!

ERIN: Dere 'mlaen

HUGH: How can I when you cadw brifo fi?

ERIN: Dewisa gerdyn arall a falle wna i stopio rhoi dolur i ti.

HUGH: I DON'T WANT TO PLAY

I WANT TO GO HOME

ERIN: Ti'n cael strop wyt ti?

HUGH: Ti'n newid y rheolau to suit you

ERIN: Wrth gwrs bo' fi'n newid y rheolau

Er mwyn siwtio fy ngêm i

Fy ngêm i yw hi

Dw i'n gallu neud beth bynnag dw i eisie

ERIN yn llyfu wyneb HUGH. HUGH yn ceisio sychu ei wyneb ei hun ond mae ei ddwylo'n dal i fod ynghlwm wrth y gadair.

HUGH: UGH

That's

hwnnan

disgusting

HOW DARE YOU

HOW DARE YOU LICK ME

Like a

Like a

Fucking

CI

Fel fucking bitch

ERIN: Ie.

Mae hi'n rhoi'r "meat hook" yn ôl yn ei le.

Nawr piga gerdyn

Oni bai bo' ti eisie i fi lyfu'r ochr arall hefyd

HUGH: Get –get your fucking spit off fy wyneb i

Y ffordd it's drying on my face

Mae'n fucking gross

ERIN: Ti'm eisie mwy?

Piga te

HUGH: Tri.

Pigo lan cerdyn arall.

ERIN: O.

Dyma gwestiwn rhyngweithiol.

ERIN yn pwyso chwarae ar Myfanwy, mae'n chwarae'r ddeialog ganlynol.

LLAIS 1: Hello?

LLAIS HUGH: Hello.

LLAIS 1: Helloooooooooooo

LLAIS HUGH: Hello!

LLAIS 1: Are you there?

LLAIS HUGH: Yes I'm here! Are you?

LLAIS 1: I'm waiting.

LLAIS HUGH: Tell me where and I'll come and find you.

LLAIS 1: Hello?

LLAIS HUGH: Yes I'm here!!

LLAIS 1: Helloooooooooooo

ERIN yn stopio'r tâp.

Saib.

ERIN: Cyfarwydd?

HUGH: *(Shrugs.)* Na

She presses play.

LLAIS 1: Hello?

LLAIS HUGH: I told you, I'm here!!

LLAIS 1: Helloooooooooooo

LLAIS HUGH: I've been waiting for ages

ERIN yn stopio'r tâp.

ERIN: Nawr?

HUGH: I've never heard that before.

Saib.

HUGH: What?

I haven't!

It's fucking weird/

Mae hi'n pwyso chwarae.

LLAIS 1: Hello?

LLAIS HUGH: I've been really looking forward to this

LLAIS 1: Helloooooooooooo

ERIN yn stopio'r tâp.

HUGH: Honestly.

I don't know what that is.

Dim yn gwybod–

I don't know who those voices belong to

But/

ERIN: Celwyddgi.

HUGH: It wasn't me –

That's not me.

ERIN: A beth yw "that" te?

Ti'n eitha pendant NID ti yw hwnna

Felly rhanna,

Beth wyt ti'n feddwl nad wyt ti wedi neud?

HUGH: I didn't understand a word of that.

ERIN: Darllena'r fucking cyfieithiad te

Beth wyt ti'n feddwl nad wyt ti wedi neud?

HUGH: Dim yn gwybod.

It's not me

I didn't/

ERIN yn chwarae ar y tâp eto.

	LLAIS HUGH: C'mon stop being such a tease.
	LLAIS 1: Are you there?
ERIN: Ai dy lais di sydd ar y tâp?	LLAIS HUGH: I can't wait to see you
Ai dy lais di sydd ar y tâp?	
Ai dy lais di sydd ar y tâp?	
ERIN yn brocio HUGH yn ei lygad.	LLAIS 1: Hello?
HUGH: AH FUCK	
I'm playing your stupid fucking game	LLAIS HUGH: Ugh don't start that again
ERIN: Ai dy lais di sydd ar y tâp?	LLAIS 1: Helloooooooooooo
Saib.	LLAIS HUGH: Please don't make me beg for it
HUGH: NO MORE	
I CAN'T/	LLAIS 1: Are you there?
Please.	

Don't make me listen to
it back.

ERIN: Ti eisie bod yn gwbwl ddall Hugh?

LLAIS HUGH: You know I want you

Ai dy lais di sydd ar y tâp?

Mae ERIN yn cydio yn wyneb HUGH ac yn mynd i brocio'r llygad arall.

LLAIS 1: Hello?

HUGH: Yes!

Mae ERIN yn stopio'r tâp. Yn dal i chwarae yn ôl y rheolau, mae'n cymryd ei hamser ac yn caniatáu sip arall o'r panda pop iddo.

ERIN: Gyda phwy wyt ti'n siarad?

HUGH: Dim yn gwybod their real name.

Just –

ERIN: Beth?

HUGH: Ugh swnio'n stupid.

ERIN: Jyst dwed e.

HUGH: Ddim ond yn gwybod-

Their username.

ERIN: Sef?

Siwr bod gen i lwy yn y drôr rhywle

'Allai'i ddefnyddio i dynnu dy lygaid di allan?

Mae'n ddigon hawdd

Mae brain yn neud e i ŵyn drwy'r amser

Jyst am ychydig o hwyl.

Nid gyda llwy wrth gwrs

Ond dw i'n siwr allai lwyddo/

HUGH: Faze.

Mae hi'n caniatáu sip arall iddo o'r panda pop.

ERIN: Os 'da ti unrhyw syniad pam wyt ti yma gyda fi nawr
    Hugh?

HUGH: No/

ERIN: Meddylia nawr

    Cyn jyst gweiddi allan

    Gei di gliw.

*Mae ERIN yn deialu rhif yn ar gyfer MYFANWY, mae'r sgrin yn
dangos galwad ffôn yn cael ei gwneud. Mae ERIN yn cerdded tuag
at HUGH ag yn tynnu ffôn sy'n canu allan o'i boced. Mae'n dangos
yr enw "FAZE" fel galwad sy'n dod i mewn.
Mae hi'n adael i'r ffonio canu allan, ag yn gadael neges arni.*

ERIN as LLAIS 1: Hello?

HUGH: What the –?

ERIN as LLAIS 1: Helloooooooooooo

HUGH: Fuck

    But you can't be Faze/

    Mae hi'n bennu y galwad ffôn.

ERIN: Bydd Erin yn neud y tro diolch

HUGH: What kind of sick person are you?

ERIN: O'n i ar fin gofyn yr un cwestiwn i ti Hugh.

HUGH: So all those chats were you the whole time?

ERIN: Ti'n deall pethe'n gyflym Hugh.

HUGH: *(Gagging.)* I – I think I'm gonna/

ERIN: Os 'allet ti geisio peidio, fyddai hynny'n wych

    Achos ei fod e'n arogli gymaint

    A fydd e'n neud i fi daflu fyny 'fyd

    A fydd llanast

A dw i ddim wir eisie gwastraffu amser yn ei lanhau

A dw i 'di rhoi gymaint o ymdrech mewn yn barod *(ERIN yn agor y drysau cefn y lladd-dy)*

I ddenu ti yma Hugh.

HUGH: Wyt ti'n some sort of glory hunter?

Well ti di fuckio fe'n barod love

Couldn't be a worse vigilante even if you tried

Achos os fi'n mynd lawr

Ti'n fucking coming with me

Meddylia what they'll do to you

Kidnapping

The mab of the Minister

ERIN: Y peth yw Hugh

Dw i ddim yn poeni am hynny Hugh

Dw i ddim yn poeni o gwbwl be naethon nhw i fi Hugh

Oherwydd mae'n rhaid i ni i gyd fynd yn y pen draw Hugh

A man a man mynd achos rhywbeth sy' werth ymladd drosto Hugh

Hugh

H-u-g-h

Syniad pwy 'odd e i sillafu fe gyda llythrennau tawel?

HUGH: I dunno

Just always spelt it that way

ERIN: Wel ti'n sillafu fe'n anghywir

Huw

bob

lliw

HUGH: Hugh every colour?

It sounded like an insult when it came out of your mouth

But I'm not sure that it is.

ERIN: Os jôc da ti pob eiliad Hugh?

ERIN yn tynnu esgidiau a sanau HUGH.

Wna i 'neud i ti chwerthin nawr

HUGH: What are you doing?

What the fuck are you doing?!

Get off me!

Get off me!

Don't you –

Don't you fucking touch me

ERIN yn dechrau ogleisio ei draed.

What?

Are you actually tickling me?

Is this a joke?

Or all part of your little domantrix bitch act?

ERIN dal yn ticlo ei draed am gyfnod anghyfforddus.

HUGH: Y peth yw Erin

I'm not into Knismolagnia

Because I'm actually not ticklish

At all

Anywhere

Never have been

ERIN: Fuck.

HUGH: Ti'm yn capable of this

I know you aren't

Fedrai gweld e in you

Ti'n rhy neis

Rhy weak

To go through with anything like this

So hwn yn ti

I know your type

ERIN: Ti ddim yn gwybod y peth cyntaf amdana i

ERIN yn chwarae y tapiau eto, maen nhw'n chwarae ar loop ac yn uwch bob tro.

Fi 'dy Faze

Fi yw'r un ti 'di bod yn siarad gyda drwy'r nos

Fi yw'r un ti 'di bod yn gofyn am luniau

Fi yw'r un oeddet ti mor awyddus i gwrdd.

> HUGH:
> Please
> I don't!
> I never really-
> I'm not what you think-
> I'll answer more questions
> I swear.

ERIN yn troi e bant.

ERIN: Dewisa cerdyn te.

HUGH: Un

ERIN: Ble oeddet ti ar yr Ugeinfed o fis Dachwedd, ddwy flynedd yn ôl?

Saib.

HUGH: I dunno.

ERIN: Nagwyt ti?

HUGH: Na

    Fi dim

    Why would I?

    I don't –

    I ugh –

    Fi dim yn cofio.

ERIN: Dw i'n mynd i ofyn i ti eto Hugh.

    Rho'r "bene-fit of the doubt"

    Fel maen nhw'n dweud.

    Ble oeddet ti ar yr Ugeinfed o fis Dachwedd, ddwy

    flynedd yn ôl?

HUGH: Fi wedi dweud,

    Dim yn cofio!

ERIN: Wyt ti'n dweud celwyddau

    Achos ti'n meddwl dw i ddim yn gwybod yn barod?

    Holl bwynt y gêm

    Yw mai ti sy'n cyfaddef.

HUGH: Confess?

    Ti'n confused.

    I haven't anything to/

ERIN: Dim bullshit Hugh

    Neu wyt ti eisie'r golau llachar 'na

    Oeddet ti'n caru gymaint nôl 'mlaen?

HUGH: Beth wyt ti eisiau me to confess?

    Rwy erioed wedi bod yn charged

Felly in the eyes of the law/

ERIN: Ond mae'r ddau ohonom

Yn gwybod yn wahanol.

A jyst achos bod y fucking algorithms,

Yn meddwl dy fod ti heb 'neud unrhywbeth

Ond ni'n gwybod y gwir

Nagyn ni?

HUGH: Beth bynnag ti'n meddwl dwi di neud

Mae'n wrong

Mae o'n guaranteed

Faultless system/

ERIN: System di-nam

I ti, falle.

Os oes gen ti rywbeth i'w guddio

Wel,

Ti'n iawn

System di-nam iawn.

HUGH: I don't

Dim byd i cuddio.

ERIN: Ble mae Gethin te?

Saib. ERIN yn syllu ar HUGH

HUGH: Beth?

ERIN: Dere 'mlan Hugh

Beth sydd gen ti i'w golli?

Gei di ymddiried ynof fi.

Saib.

Tair mlynedd yn ôl *(Storm y tu allan yn gwaethygu'n raddol)*

Dechreuodd Fragger siarad ar lein gyda Destroyer

Daethon nhw'n agos iawn

Yn gyflym iawn.

'Wedodd Destroyer wrth Fragger

Ei fod e'n deall yn union beth mae fel i fod yn unig,

Heb ffrindiau,

I gael Tad sy'n brifo pawb

Y bullshit 'ma i gyd

A dechrau rhywfath o-

Nath Destroyer perswadio Fragger

I gwrdd

I chwarae

Ar noson yr ugainfed o Dachwedd

Mi oedd Fragger yn disgwyl cwrdd â bachgen arall

Ond pwy oedd 'na?

Ti.

Dyn

Bron yn ei dridegau

Dyn oedd wedi

"Grwmio"

fy mab

HUGH: Your son?

ERIN: Ie, mab fi!

A dw i eisie gwybod pob ffaith manwl

O'r diwrnod aeth e

Sut

Pryd

A pham

Gwed!

Neu wnest ti fwrw bachgen bach saith mlwydd oed

Dros ei ben

A'i gario i ffwrdd hefyd?

Dw i 'di bod yn aros

Gorwedd yn effro

Sefyll yn y baw

Methu anadlu

Am ddwy flynedd nawr

Am ateb diriaethol

Os ydy fy mab i dal yn fyw

A dw i byth wedi bod yn un

I aros yn ddistaw neu'n gwrtais

Felly penderfynais wneud rhywbeth

Does dim byd arall i mi golli

Ma' fy mab wedi diflannu

A'r unig peth odd ar ôl

Odd y sgyrsiau gawsoch chi

Wedi'u safio ar ei gyfrifiadur

Gymrest di bopeth oddi wrtha i.

A dyma ti nawr

Mewn fucking ladd-dŷ gyda fi.

Felly dwed wrtha i

Jyst dwed

Ble ma' Gethin?

Saib.

Ble ma' Gethin?

Ble ma' Gethin?

Ble ma' Gethin?

Hugh

Ble ma' Gethin?

Ble ma' Gethin?

Ble ma' Gethin?

Ble ma' Gethin?

Mae hi'n dal ei fawd gyda'r bwriad i'w dorri.

HUGH:AH/

Yn sydyn mae sgrech uchel, ERIN yn cwmpo i'r llawr.

ERIN: na na na na na na na na

LLAIS Distorted ERIN: Mae'n ddrwg gen i i dorri ar draws ond mae gen i gais ar frys

Mae'n ddrwg gen i

Plentyn

Plentyn/

ERIN: GETHIN/

LLAIS DISTORTED ERIN: Mae'n ddrwg gen i i dorri ar draws ond mae gen i gais ar frys am blentyn ar goll

Mae'r sgrech yn stopio. ERIN yn cymryd anadl ddofn, mae hi'n gwybod na all hi ildio i'r foment honno, mae ganddi swydd i'w gwneud nawr.

ERIN: Ti'n sychedig?

Ti'n edrych yn sychedig

Ti eisie diod arall?

YFA

NAWR

Mae hi'n gorfodi'r panda pop i'w geg.

Mae'n yfed.

Mae'n ceisio stopio ond nid yw ERIN yn ei symud i
ffwrdd fel o'r blaen. Mae hi eisiau iddo yfed y cyfan.

Ti'n gweld

Mae 'na un peth

Fel rhiant

Dw i'n casau fy hunan am wneud yn y sefyllfa yma,

Dw i'n mynd drosodd a throsodd

Pob eiliad

Yn trial dadansoddi

Yr holl sefyllfa

Sut allwn i fod wedi ei ddysgu

I fyth ymddiried mewn dieithryn.

Ond bob tro

Mae'n dod nôl at y ffaith dy fod ti'n oedolyn

A ddylet ti wybod yn well

Achos rwyt ti newydd orffen

Cymysgedd o panda pop

A shit load o Fentanyl

A be ti'n profi nawr

Yw artaith fferyllol

Sef

Y defnydd o gyffuriau

I gosbi

Neu i dynnu

Gwybodaeth allan o berson

Felly os wyt ti eisie byw

Hugh

Well i ti gydweithio

Ac ateb fucking cwestiwn fi

BLE

MAE

GETHIN?

Saib.

Mae ymwybyddiaeth HUGH yn dechrau newid.

Adleisir hyn gydag ystumiad o'r storm y tu allan.

HUGH: If you do kill me

Even if you do

Ti

You can't

Stopio

This

Hwn

The cycle

The algo

Fucking

Rhythyms

Y cylch

They've got him.

Achos

There's more

And they're –

Especially…

HUGH yn sylweddoli'r hyn yr oedd ar fin ei ddweud..

Mae'r glaw yn mynd yn drymach, mae yna daran isel o daranau yn y pellter.

ERIN: Beth?

'Especially' beth?

Saib.

'Especially' fucking beth?

'Especially' fucking BETH Hugh?!

HUGH: NHW

Y cylch/

ERIN: Beth yw'r cylch/

HUGH groans.

ERIN: BLE MAE GETHIN?

PLIS

Dw i ddim eisie dy ladd di

Dw i jyst eisie Gethin nôl

Dy dro di yw hi i wneud y peth iawn Hugh

Dyma dy gyfle di

I fod yn berson da

Wyt ti am ei gymryd e?

Saib – Mae HUGH bron yn anymwybodol o'r cyffur i wneud unrhyw synnwyr.

ERIN: Fuck sake Hugh

Mae hi'n ei smacio.

Dihuna!

ERIN: FOR FUCK SAKE!

Cerddoriaeth.

LLAIS ERIN: 'Dyw e dal ddim wedi dod nôl

LLAIS DYN: Dw i wedi gweud wrthot ti, mae ein tîm ar y ffordd i neud arolygiadau

LLAIS ERIN: Dwyt ti ddim yn deall, 'odd e fod gartref oriau yn ôl.

LLAIS DYN: Dw i'n siwr bod e dal allan yn chwarae. Wyt ti wedi checio pob perthynas sydd ganddo fe? Beth am ei Dad?

LLAIS ERIN: Na! 'Dyw e byth wedi bod yn rhan o'i fywyd. Ma rhywbeth yn bod a dwyt ti ddim yn gwrando arna i!

LLAIS DYN: Mae'n ddrwg gen i Ms ond mae'n rhaid i chi dawelu, does dim angen gweiddi, chi braidd yn hysterig. Mae hwn yn rhan o'r weithdrefn.

LLAIS ERIN: Dw i ddim! Mae rhywbeth o'i le, dw i jyst yn gwybod.

LLAIS DYN: Dw i'n siwr bydd popeth yn iawn. Fel arfer mae nhw jyst wedi rhedeg i rywle, wnawn ni ffeindio fe.

LLAIS ERIN: Pam dwyt ti ddim yn gwrando arna i?

LLAIS DYN: Dw i yn, ond mae'n fachgen ifanc. Dw i'n cofio pan o'n i ei oedran e…

LLAIS ERIN: Galwa fe'n reddf mamol. Ond mae rhywbeth yn fucking bod!

WOMAN: Mae'n annhebygol iawn y caiff eich achos ei brosesu ymhellach.

mae'n annhebygol iawn y caiff eich achos ei brosesu ymhellach.

mae'n annhebygol iawn y caiff eich achos ei brosesu ymhellach.

mae'n annhebygol iawn y caiff eich achos ei brosesu ymhellach.

mae'n annhebygol iawn y caiff eich achos ei brosesu ymhellach.

ERIN yn ysgwyd ei phen, ni all ei gredu.

Rydyn ni'n gweld ERIN yn ail-fyw'r eiliad y darganfu fod ei phlentyn wedi diflannu. Gall hyn fod yn llythrennol neu trwy'r defnydd o symudiad.

ERIN: Rhaid dy fod ti dal 'ma.

WOMAN: Diolch i chi am eich pryder ac am gymryd yr amser i gadw'ch gwlad yn ddiogel.

PEDWAR

Awr neu ddwy yn ddiweddarach.

Mae ERIN yn eistedd o'i flaen yn bwyta ffa-pob o dun ffa pob.

ERIN: Dere 'mlan

Mae hi'n codi i edrych ar ei anadlu.

Fucking coda

Fucking prick.

Mae hi'n syllu arno ac yna'n ei gwthio.

Mae HUGH yn rhoi griddfan isel.

ERIN: Croeso nôl atom ni

Gest di nap neis?

Prin gall agor ei lygaid na dal ei ben i fyny, griddfan isel arall.

ERIN: Ti nôl gyda ni'n iawn?

Ti'n gallu siarad?

Hugh?

HUGH!

HUGH grunts.

ERIN: Wyt ti'n gallu agor dy lygaid?

Ti angen bach o siwgr?

Falle bod gen i Milky-way yn rhywle.

Mae hi'n dod o hyd i "funsize Milky-way". Mae hi'n ei ddadlapio.

ERIN: Cymer peth

HUGH methu cymrud unrhywbeth.

Mae hi'n torri hanner uchaf y siocled i ffwrdd.

ERIN: Rhaid i ti ei sugno

Paid cnoi

Mae hi'n gosod y slab bach o siocled yn ei geg.
Gyda'i bys mae'n rhoi e yn ceg HUGH, mae HUGH yn ceisio ei brathu, ond yn methu yn unig.

ERIN: Fucking bastard

Nest di drial cnoi fi?

Saib.

ERIN: Nest di drial fucking cnoi fi?

Ti'n gi sy'n cnoi pobl wyt ti?

Wyt ti'n gwybod be ni'n neud

Gyda cŵn sy'n fucking cnoi pobl

Ar y fferm?

HUGH yn poeri yn ei hwyneb hi.

ERIN: *(Wiping it off calmly.)* Ti'n meddwl bo' bach o boer

Yn mynd i droi fi bant?

Ar ôl cymaint o amser?

Pa mor bell?

Bach yn rhy hwyr am hwnna

Nag wyt ti'n meddwl?

Ni'n

"in too deep"

Fel maen nhw'n dweud.

ERIN yn bwyta'r milkyway.

Saib.

HUGH: Pam nes di ddim lladd fi when you had the chance?

ERIN: Odd 'na foment pan feddyliais i wneud hynny

Ond

Yn y pendraw

Mae marwolaeth yn rhy rhwydd i ti

Gei di ddechrau eto mewn marwolaeth

Ac os mae'n rhaid i mi gario 'mlaen

Crwydro drwy'r cachu yma bob dydd

Yn sicr,

Does dim hawl 'da ti i adael,

Does dim hawl 'da ti i anghofio pwy wyt ti

Well gen i

Dy fod ti'n dioddef gyda fi

HUGH: Ti'n neud iddo swnio

Fel dylai dweud

Diolch/

Neu bod yn

Grateful

Fucking grateful am dim ond

Kidnapping me

Tying me up

Pulling my arm hairs out

Water boarding me

Kicking me in the bollocks

Trying to tickle me

Poking me in the eye

And

Drugging me

OH

Diolch fucking byth

ERIN: Bach yn anniolchgar

Os wyt ti'n gofyn i fi

Allwn i jyst dy ladd di'n syth

HUGH: Newch e then!

So diwrnod yn pasio

Where I don't think about letting the river

Just fucking swallow me anyway

ERIN: Ti'n meddwl ti yw'r unig un?

Ti'n meddwl ti yw'r unig un sy'n dioddef?

Rhaid dy fod ti'n sylweddoli

Fod popeth ti 'di neud

Yn cael effaith

Yn effeithio ar bobl

Bywydau pobl

Calonnau pobl

Teuluoedd pobl

HUGH: Falle ti'n iawn

I dunno

Falle dwi just ddim yn deall e

Falle dwi just methu –

Comprehend –

Saib.

Ugh

I've always known I was/

That I wanted/

Ugh

Sain siwr

Falle

O'n i'n

Bored.

Odd e'n hawdd

Odd e'n hawdd perswadio

'Na beth oedd "ffrindiau" yn wneud.

Dau ohonynt yn eistedd yn y wybodaeth hon.

ERIN: Dechreuaist di

Achos oeddet ti'n

Ddiflas?

HUGH: Fi'n meddwl

Ie –

Falle.

ERIN: Dw i ddim yn dy gredu di.

Os oeddet ti'n ddiflas

Dylet ti 'di ffeindio fucking hobi.

HUGH: Erin,

I know it's awful

Ond dwi methu undo what I've done

But dwi gallu helpu ti nawr

Meddyliwch

Os neu di adael fi mynd…

Nawr

Fedrai

Actually

Helpu di.

ERIN: Rwyt ti wedi helpu digon.

HUGH: Wi'n sori Erin

Ife na be ti ishe glywed?

Ife na be ti angen

I adael i fi mynd?

ERIN: NA

DWYT TI DDIM YN DEALL

Dw i ddim eisie dy ymddiheuriad

Dw i eisie gwybod ble mae Gethin

HUGH: Mae na siawns/

ERIN: Fuck

HUGH: Wnai gweud/

ERIN: Ble mae e?

HUGH: Os wyt ti'n untie-o fi.

Falle neiff e all come flooding back.

ERIN: Bullshit

HUGH: Iawn

Have it your way

Ond trust me

Wnai ddim dweud unrhywbeth arall

Tan wyt ti'n gadael fi mynd

Saib.

ERIN: Dw i ddim yn afresymol.

Ti'n addo,

Ar fywyd dy deulu-

Y byddi di'n dweud popeth

A dw i'n meddwl fucking popeth

Rwyt ti'n gwybod

Am Gethin,

Ei leoliad –

A wna i adael i ti fynd.

HUGH: Addo.

ERIN: Dwed e te.

Yn ffurfiol

Yn y ffordd

Gyfreithiol

Dere addo,

Gan gynnwys yr "whole truth and nothing but the truth",

Nawr!

HUGH: I swear in the name of God that what I shall state shall be the truth, the whole truth and nothing but the truth.

Saib. ERIN yn sefyll yn union o flaen ei wyneb, yn ei atgoffa o'r dasg o'i flaen.

HUGH: It is most likely mae nhw wedi symud Gethin ymlaen.

ERIN: Mae e dal yn fyw?

HUGH: As far as I'm aware

Ie.

ERIN: I KNEW IT

'Nes i byth stopio meddwl

Ei fod e dal yn fyw

Ble mae e?

HUGH: Dw i ddim yn gwybod

ERIN: Ti ddim yn gwybod?

Sut wyt ti ddim yn gwybod?

HUGH: YOU SAID YOU'D UNTIE ME

ERIN: Dy ddatglymu di am 'it's most likely'?

Dw i ddim yn meddwl/

HUGH: WEDES DI

YOU CAN'T LIE ERIN

YOU SAID

AND I DELIVERED

PAID BOD YN CELWIDDGI

Wedes di

Ti ddim yn chwarae'n iawn/

ERIN: Paid siarad i fi am be sy'n deg

Pam wyt ti ddim yn gwybod?!

HUGH: Odd rhaid i fi rhoi Gethin fyny

Erin

Fi'n gwybod sut mae'n swnio

Ond odd rhaid i fi talu'r pris

I sicrhau

Subtlety a silence

Odd rhaid i fi

Odd dim dewis arall gyda fi

I had to protect my own

You've no idea how difficult a decision it was

Gorfod –

Having to give him up

Erin

Mae'r dau ohynyn ni'n edyrch am e/

ERIN: Ti wir yn trial hi on'd wyt ti

Meiddia fucking di

'Dyw'r ddau ohonom ni ddim yn chwilio 'da'n gilydd

Dy' ni ddim yn dîm

Ti'n ffiaidd

A ti sy' 'di difetha'm mywyd i

Dy ddatglymu di am senario

"it's most likely"

Mae hynny'n fucking bullshit

Dw i'n mynd i dy fucking ladd di

Pam dwyt ti ddim yn gwybod?

Ble mae e?

Ti oedd yr un 'nath ei ddenu,

Groomed.

HUGH: LOVED

ERIN: PAID TI A FUCKING MENTRO/

HUGH: When they took him from me/

ERIN yn gafael ynddo ac yna'n cydio yn ei wyneb, gan geisio ei fygu, ond nad yw hi'n dda iawn.

ERIN: Dw i ddim eisie'i glywed

Dw i ddim eisie clywed dy "pity party" di

Fi yw ei Fam e

A fi'n gwybod na fydde fe 'di mynd yn gwbwl fodlon 'da ti,

Dw i'n nabod fy mab i

Ti 'nath ei fucking ddwyn e

Ti 'nath ddwyn fy mhlentyn oddi wrtha i

Ti 'nath ddwyn plentyn oddi wrth ei Fam

O'i gartref

Rhwygo fe wrtha i pan o'dd fy nghefn i wedi'i droi.

A phan na ddaeth e nôl,

Fucking hell on earth began

And my womb screams for him every fucking second

Because he is a part of me

He's my every single thought

And he is all that I have

And I will shout and scream until I know that he's safe

Nôl gartref

Ble mae fucking fod

Hwnna 'dy cariad.

Nawr dwed ble fuck mae e

Nawr

Neu dw i'n addo i fucking Dduw wnai/

She breaks and collapses.

Dylai rhwygo dy fucking dafod allan.

Eisteddwn yn y foment hon tra bod HUGH yn dal ei anadl.

HUGH: Erin

Dw i'n sori.

But you have to know

Mae hwn

Y cylch

Their control

Mae'n lot fwy na just fi.

They took him from me.

ERIN: "They"?

"Y Cylch"?

Wedest di

"You can't stop the cycle."

Wedest di

"There's more"

Pwy oeddet ti'n feddwl?

HUGH: Erin/

ERIN: Pwy yw 'nhw'?

HUGH: Shut up and I'll tell you.

Ond

Mae'n rhaid i ti

Addo

Neu di adael fi mynd

A wnai just

Diflannu

Mae ERIN yn codi'r rubix cube, yn ei barhau wrth iddi feddwl am y fargen hon.

Mae'n gwblhau, ei roi yn ôl ar y bwrdd

ERIN: Iawn 'te

Dwed

HUGH: Bots 'ma

Yr algorithms.

Mae'n propaganda

To make you believe its for convenience.

They've been programmed,

Ensuring protection for this "select" group

And this group is growing

Ar pob level

Mae na fwy a fwy o bobl mewn arno fe

Heddlu

Judges

Politicians

Pawb yn helpu ei gilydd

You scratch my back,

And we'll help you seek out the vulnerable.

Meetings

Sex parties

Burning down the buildings afterwards

Destroying the evidence

Enwi fo

Neithen nhw helpu

Os mae'r pris yn iawn.

Generally it's pictures,

Ond mae'n rhaid fod nhw heb gweld nhw o'r blaen

Neu os ma fwy o peryg

Something of equivalent value.

Ag os mae rhywun

Neu rhywbeth

Slips through the net

Falle fod rhywun yn ffeindio'r nerth

I dod ymlaen

They are miraculously found dead before they get to testify

These algorithms are put in place

I cadw ni,

Y cylch

Pawb

Yn ein lle

A dwi just yn fucking pawn,

Son of The Minister,

Under the thumb,

Dwi'n/

Nothing

A mae nhw'n neud hynnyn realli fucking glir

They won't even give a shit that you've killed me.

If they knew you had me tied up

They'd just delete our entire existence

In the click of a finger

Because it's much much bigger Erin

Yn lot fwy na just tying me to a fucking chair

Saib.

ERIN: Y gwir yw hwn?

Pam ddylwn i dy gredu di?

HUGH: Dunno

I suppose s'dim rhaid i ti

Ond what else have you got

To get you closer to Gethin?

ERIN: Fucking

Nhw i gyd

Gwneud eu hun yn gyfforddus

HUGH: Ie

Yr eiliad someone gets brave

They'll defend them until the end

"Oh no they couldn't possibly

So nhw'n fath na o berson

Ma nhw'n rhy neis

They contribute so much to our society

They couldn't possibly"

Ond mae'n celwyddau

Wrth gwrs

I amddiffyn ein gilydd.

It doesn't matter how good you paint yourself to others,

Everybody is capable of darkness

ERIN: A ti

Ti'n ffiaidd

Ond dwi i'n mynd i hela pob un ohonoch chi

Saib. ERIN yn dechrau paratoi i adael, mae hi'n codi waled HUGH o'r ddesg.

HUGH: WAIT

Where are you going?

You said you'd let me go!

You can just leave me here

ERIN: 'Na'n union be dw i'n mynd i'w wneud'

Achos dw i eisie i ti ddioddef

Yn araf

Ac yn boenus

Felly dw i am adael i ti bydru

Dw i am neud i ti ddeall be mae fel –

HUGH: Beth y fuck wyt ti'n meddwl?

ERIN: Wel

I fod yn hollol onest

Mae na un peth

Dw i ddim yn deall

Felly

Awn ni nôl ychydig

Am rhywfaint o gyd-destun

Ife?

Mae gen ti deulu

Ferch

Dy hun

Sut allet ti fodoli

A gwneud y pethau rwyt ti wedi ei wneud

I waed dy hunain?

HUGH: No she's my daughter

Of course not

ERIN: Dim ond plant pobl eraill te?

HUGH: I know how it sounds –

ERIN: Wyt ti'n Dadi gwych te Hugh?

Saib.

Gei di feddwl am y peth os wyt ti eisie

Drosodd a throsodd

Coledda'r atgofion

Dychmyga

Achos rydyn ni am ddod

I ryw fath o fargen

Plentyn am blentyn

Mae hi'n ei agor i fyny ac yn dal llun.

Ti 'di bod yn eu helpu nhw

Cyfrannu at yr achos

A nawr

Rwyt ti am dalu am y peth

Wna i dalu am Gethin

A ymdreiddio'r sefydliad o tu fewn y cylch

A talu'r pris

Efo Mable

Dangos y llun sydd ganddi yw o Mable.

HUGH: Na

Erin

Gad hi fod

ERIN: Mae'n beth pert iawn nagyw hi

HUGH: Leave her out of this

ERIN: Rhy hwyr am hynny

Bydd Modryb Erin yn ei chasglu hi o'r ysgol

O ddosbarth Mrs Andrews/

HUGH: HOW DO YOU KNOW THAT/

ERIN: Ac awn ni am daith bach

A stopio am dê yn FcDonalds/

HUGH: Don't you dare!/

ERIN: Achos ei bod hi'n caru eu teganau nhw

Nagyw hi?/

HUGH: Like the fuck am I going to tell you/

ERIN: A gall hi fwyta ei 'nuggets' cyw iâr

Tra ein bod ni ar y ffordd/

HUGH: Very fucking funny Erin,

You've had your joke now/

ERIN: I ffeindio y cylch, o cylch hosana 'ma/

HUGH: NO

ERIN DON'T

IT WON'T WORK

THEY'LL KILL YOU

AND TAKE HER

NO HESITATION/

ERIN: Mae drosodd Hugh

'Sdim byd arall alli di weud

Dw i'n mynd i adael i ti bydru fan hyn

Ond tra bo' ti'n pydru

Meddylia am y ffaith

'Dyw person fel ti

Ddim yn haeddu cael

Cariad pur plentyn

Dwyt ti ddim yn haeddu cael y pleser

77

Y dyfnder, o'r cariad diddiwedd a diderfyn.

'Sdim teimlad arall sy'n dod yn agos ato

HUGH: SHUT THE FUCK UP

WHO THE FUCK ARE YOU TO DECIDE!

IF YOU TOUCH MABLE I'LL

I'LL FUCKING/

ERIN: Fucking beth Hugh?

Ti 'di clymu i fyny

HUGH: Don't fucking test me Erin

Wnai fucking ladd ti

STAY AWAY FROM HER/

ERIN: Y peth yw Hugh,

Ti'n beryglus

Ti 'di dweud e dy hunan

A dw i'n methu gadael rhywun

Sy'n fygythiad i'n cymdeithas,

Allan yn rhydd

Fydde hwnna'n anghyfrifol.

HUGH: Ti methu neud hwn

YOU CAN'T TAKE MABLE

Ti'n fucking mental

ERIN: Ydw dw i yn "fucking mental"

Wyt ti'n deall nawr?

Nawr bod bygythiad

Falle neu di golli'r person

Rwyt ti'n ei charu fwyaf yn y byd

Falle nawr

Yn yr eiliad yma

Rwyt ti'n dechrau deall

Yr effaith

Beth wyt ti wir wedi ei wneud

HUGH: NO

YOU BITCH

NO

YOU CAN'T TAKE HER

YOU CAN'T

I WONT LET YOU

I WONT FUCKING LET YOU

ERIN yn troi i adael, gan wybod beth sy'n rhaid iddi ei wneud. HUGH yn cael'n rhydd ac yn torri'n rhydd, mae'n dal ERIN ag yn tagu hi o'r tu ôl.

HUGH: Dylai fucking ladd ti

Grumble isel o daranau. Rydyn ni'n clywed seirenau. Mae ERIN yn dechrau ymladd yn ol ag yn geisio cael'n rhydd.

HUGH: Beth?

O ti wir yn meddwl,

Ferch bach fel ti

Fydd ddim consequences?

Fedre ddim just adael i ti cael get away

Oh – yn enwedig achos fod nhw reit tu fas.

Seirenau'n dod yn agosach.

Achos pan ma nhw'n weld fod ti di herwgipio

Fi

(Da ni'n gwybod yn barod Erin

Newn nhw ddim gredu

79

unrhywbeth ti'n gweud)

A wnai weud

Odd e'n self defence

POLICEV/O: Heddlu, agorwch i fyny.   *The door is continuously being banged on.*

ERIN yn llwyddo i cael'n rhydd, mae hi'n cydio yn y ddyfais castration "All in One" ac yn ei daro dros ei ben - gan ei guro'n ddisynnwyr. Y stormydd yn tanlinellu.
Mae'r canlynol yn digwydd ochr yn ochr â'r V / O ar yr un pryd.

ERIN V/O:
Nad os eiliad yn pasio

Mae'r dilyniant canlynol wedi'i steilio. Pan dw i ddim yn
gwrando i'r sibrwd

Mae ERIN yn tynnu'r trowsus a'r pants Y newyn yn fy mhen
bant o HUGH .
 Y trymder yn fy stumog i
(Mewn ffordd sy'n awgrymu Sy'n dweud,
i'r gynulleidfa ond NID yw'n Rwyt ti dal yma
hanfodol ein bod ni'n gweld
noethni) Achos 'sdim dewis 'da fi
ERIN yn pwyso mewn , ni'n Mae'n rhaid i fi dy
clywed pop a mae HUGH yn ffeindio di
sgrechian. A dod â ti nôl adre'
 A phan dy fod ti nôl Fe
ERIN wedi ei ysbaddu. gofleidia'i di gyda'r holl
Mae hi'n dal ei follocks. gariad sydd gen i

POLICE V/O: Agorwch y drws! A'th garu am byth
bythoedd

Agorwch i fyny nawr! Ect.
Drysau yn agor.

CHILD V/O: Mami?

Mae ERIN yn troi gyda bollocks HUGH yn ei law, wedi'u gorchuddio yn gwaed.

ERIN: Fuck

SNAP BLACKOUT

HELA
Translation

Un

A flood of music.

It's glitchy we see on the AV:

WOMAN: Thank you/ ON THE AV: algorithm - algərɪð(ə)m/

Only/	"a process / broses
10%	or set of rules / neu set o reolau
10%	to be followed in calculations or other problem-solving operations, /
10%	i'w ddilyn mewn cyfrifiadau neu weithrediadau datrys problemau eraill,
Possibility/	especially by a computer./
So/	yn enwedig gan gyfrifiadur."

It's unlikely/

VOICE: Welcome to X Land. You told us that you're visiting for X days.

We'd like to remind you that there will be consequences if you extend your stay without permission

Glitches. SNAP MUSIC OFF A BLACKOUT.

We are now in an abattoir. Everything inside the abattoir is from a different decade, as if it's a hand me down. There's papers in amongst other mess across the floor, the papers have been torn up, as if there's been a big bust up.

We notice HUGH, who is unconscious, with blood on his forehead, tied to a chair.

Snap to an incredibly strong spot light on HUGH. This wakes him.

HUGH: Ah.

That's really –

Shit.

That's bright

I can't…

We hear footsteps.

Enter ERIN – dressed in a pair dungarees.

ERIN: Hello?

HUGH: Hello! YES!

I'm over here

Please HELP!

ERIN: What the – ?

Oh my god

HUGH: Oh fuck

Quickly!

That light.

It's really hurting my eyes!

Can you turn it off?

ERIN stands in front of the spot light, her silhouette is shading HUGH's eyes.

HUGH: That's a little better

But if you could just/

ERIN: Are you alright?

HUGH: I don't know what you're saying

Can you just turn that light off/

ERIN: Are you alright?

HUGH: Jesus

Just turn the light off will you/

ERIN: What are you doing here?

HUGH looks down at his wrists noticing he's tied up.

HUGH: Fuck

Help

Please

Help

You have to get me out of here

ERIN: Is there somebody that wants to hurt you or
something?

HUGH: Is that ugh/

Are you speaking/

I'm sorry

But I don't speak/

ERIN: Who did this to you?

HUGH: I – *(Trying to move.)*

I really don't know what you're saying

So please

Just help me

I'm begging you

I'm fucking tied up for Christ sake

Someone's tied me up/

ERIN quickly checks moving out of the light, HUGH winces.

HUGH: AH Fuck! Please

That light –

It's

ERIN: Ye

You're tied up

Pretty tight aswell

ERIN stand in front of the light again.

ERIN: Better?

HUGH: I guess that's helping

But if you could untie me

That would be so much better

And then I can/

ERIN turns off the light and goes to inspect them further.

ERIN: They're handcuffs.

Is there a key?

HUGH: Please.

I don't know what you're saying

Or how else to say it

Just untie me will you.

UN-TIE M-E

ERIN: I need a key

HUGH: Ugh god

I don't know how else to say it.

ERIN: KEY

I NEED A KEY

HUGH: Is that your name?

I don't know any Ac-wed

ERIN: No

KEY

"LL"

Like the sound a cat makes

KEY

HUGH: Is that your name?

ERIN demonstrates a key.

ERIN: KEY

HUGH: Oh

Key.

Then just say it in Eng/

ERIN grabs HUGH's face, there's a playfulness.

HUGH: What the/

ERIN: They're not a huge fan of that language in here

She's just holding his face, staring at it. Playfulness drops, we think she wants to kiss him.

Releasing his face with a slight pat and a smile.

Just trying to help…

Lifting his floppy hair with her finger, a demureness.

We'll have to clean that.

ERIN finds a glass of what we presume is water. She dips her fingers in and then touches the wound on his forehead. He winces.

HUGH: Please

Is that water?

Can I have some/

She dips her fingers in and then touches the wound on his forehead. He winces.

HUGH: AH

Jesus

What is that?

ERIN: Vodka

HUGH: Surely you can't be old enough to be drinking that/

ERIN: Is it painful?

Your cut?

HUGH: I'm sorry

But you clearly understand what I'm saying

So why are you still choosing to talk at me in/

ERIN: You don't even understand a little bit?

HUGH: "Bach"!

Bach is little isn't it?

ERIN: So you do understand?

Or are you a little deaf?

HUGH: "Tipyn bach"

Is that right?

I can't speak it anymore see.

ERIN: And by now you've forgotten?

You've been running for too long

And reconsidered who you are?

Changed you accent

BLAH BLAH BLAH

The same old bullshit

HUGH: All I got from that was blahblahblah, bullshit.

ERIN: Do you want to understand?

Perhaps there is a way…

Pause.

Do you want to understand

Hugh?

HUGH: How do you know my name?

ERIN: Do you want to understand?

HUGH: How the fuck do you know my name?!

ERIN: I'm asking you a question

And you have to answer

   Or they'll be angry

HUGH: Cwestiwn

   Question

   Right?

   A slow hand clap.

ERIN: Congrats Hedd Wyn

   You're basically fluent now.

Would you like to understand?

HUGH: Whatever it is you're asking –

   It feels like you want me to say yes.

ERIN: Yes I do.

HUGH: And if I don't –

   Because you do realise

I don't know what I'm agreeing to/

ERIN: You can find out if you'd like

   But it'll be a lot easier for everyone if you

   Just give us an answer

HUGH: I'm not being funny

   But

Who even are you?

ERIN: I got sent to help you

But you don't even understand

What I'm saying

So what's the point/

HUGH: How old are you?

ERIN: Guess!

HUGH: I think you're probably a

Teenager

Maybe

But I don't know how many times I have to say this to you

I do not know what you are asking me to agree to

Do you understand that?

ERIN: Do you want to understand or not?

Do you want to understand?

Answer me.

Do you want to understand?

Do you want to understand/

HUGH: Yes?

ERIN: Yes I do

HUGH: Yes.

ERIN: Yes I do

HUGH: Yes.

ERIN: You have to say "Yes I do"

Say "Yes I do"

"Yes I do"

Saying it slowly.

UH-DW

Pause.

HUGH: UH-DW

ERIN: Then let's start again shall we

"MYFANWY" translate for Hugh

ERIN reveals a Alexa type device and from here on subtitles are shown in English.

ERIN: Is it painful?

HUGH registers that he can now read the translation on the TV.

HUGH: How is it/

ERIN: Your cut/

HUGH: Doing that?

ERIN: Is it still painful?

HUGH: Yes.

Stinging.

How have you managed that?

How is it translating like that/

ERIN: Shame.
(She "accidentally" throws the dregs of vodka in his face.)

HUGH: WHAT THE-

FUCK!

AHHHHHHHH

IT'S IN

MY EYES

FUCK.

ERIN: Oh I'm so sorry

I feel awful

Sorry

But at least

It's cleaning your cut/

HUGH trying and failing to wipe away the liquid from his eyes.

HUGH: UGH YOU –

FOR FUCK SAKE

I can't wipe my fucking eyes because of these fucking/

ERIN: Oh whoops

I didn't think of that

Sorry

Sorry

Sorry

ERIN wipes his face dry – an act of affection.

ERIN: *(Whisper.)* But you've just swore in front of me

And they wouldn't like that

HUGH: What

No

I didn't mean it

It was just because of the vodka in my eyes

Am I a hostage?

ERIN: No

The word "hostage" doesn't suit you.

HUGH: What's that supposed to mean/

ERIN: Who are you then?

HUGH: Did they tell you my name?

Or are you like Twelve or Eleven or whatever her name is?

ERIN: Of course they told me

But I'm not asking you what your name is.

I'm asking,

Who are you?

Hugh.

Pause.

HUGH: Let's be honest

It's not like it's hard to find out

To be fair

My Dad is

Well

My Dad

After all

ERIN: Ye

I suppose

HUGH: So they told you?

You know,

For a girl your age

I would have thought you'd have figured it out yourself

ERIN: Use the internet you mean?

Because people my age are obsessed with the internet

Aren't they.

I'm being detained here exactly like you

HUGH: But you do know who I am

Right?

ERIN: Ye

They told me

HUGH: You keep saying "they"

Who are they?

And what do they want with me?

ERIN: *(Shrugs her shoulder.)*

They

I'm not really sure.

I just do what they tell me

Otherwise I'll never be free

HUGH: Is that how this works?

   If I do what they say they'll let me go

ERIN: I suppose

HUGH: So there's a chance I can get out?

   ERIN: Possibly - I've heard stories

   But I think they killed the last boy who tried

   So who knows

HUGH: Fuck

   Okay

   Okay

   How do I get them to let me go?

   Or at least untie me?

ERIN: Not really sure to tell you the truth

HUGH: Fuck

ERIN: Stop swearing is probably a good place to start

HUGH: How did you get out of your chains?

ERIN: Sitting quietly

HUGH: Okay I can do that

ERIN: For a week

HUGH: Okay no I can't do that

ERIN: Fine then

   Sit in those cuffs until the end of time

   Suit yourself

   ERIN goes to leave.

HUGH: NO NO PLEASE

COME BACK

I'll do anything

Please

ERIN: Anything?

If it was up to me

Honestly, I would have already

But they wouldn't be very pleased

If they found out

Another prisoner let you free

But would you really do anything?

Because if it was worth my time…

HUGH: Yes

Anything

Please

Don't make me beg

ERIN: Fine.

I'll wait then.

HUGH: For me to beg?

ERIN: No

I'll wait here

I'll help you

If you agree to do what I want.

HUGH: Okay

Anything you need

Pause.

ERIN: I'll exchange that promise when I'm ready.

Ha

That rhymed

HUGH: So are you a prisoner too?

ERIN: Yes

HUGH: I didn't realise you were

ERIN: Well, I just told you

HUGH: No I mean until you just said that

What are you/ (in for?)

ERIN: What made you assume that?

HUGH: Well/

ERIN: Is it because I'm a younger than you

That I couldn't possibly

Or because I'm attractive/

HUGH: *(Snigger.)* You think a lot of yourself don't you/

ERIN: Why shouldn't I think a lot of myself?

You think a lot of yourself

Without me judging you/

HUGH: Christ

That's not what I meant

ERIN: Why couldn't I be a prisoner then?

HUGH: No no I didn't mean it like/

You can

If you want to

It's just that logistically/

ERIN: There's no way

You could be sharing a cell

With a girl

My age

HUGH: Well yes…

Pause.

She picks up a rubix cube that is placed on her desk.

ERIN: I've been trying to solve this for two years.

And I think tonight, I will.

HUGH: It's taken you two years to solve a puzzle?

ERIN: Ye

Why?

HUGH: It's just –

I don't really give a shit about your rubix cube

I need you to help me escape

ERIN: Did you know,

On average it takes

About twenty moves to finish a rubix cube?

I've got about three moves left, Hugh

HUGH: You aren't even listening to me

How old even are you?

ERIN: Old enough to understand why I'm here.

HUGH: What?

ERIN: We're here because of our decisions Hugh.

Their results.

You are here,

Because of your own decisions.

HUGH is speechless.

HUGH: My own decisions?

ERIN: Oh don't be like that Hugh

HUGH: I didn't decide to tie myself to a chair

ERIN: No

I tied you

But I had to tie you up

Firstly, because they told me to

And then because I was afraid you would hurt yourself

And that you wouldn't listen

I know you don't believe me

Your face isn't very good at hiding it

But to prove it

You can know a little about me

My name is Erin

I'm a farmer's daughter

And I'm now single

All on my own

Just me

People think I'm totally crazy

And maybe they're right

I don't blame them

Now

A little game to pass the time?

HUGH: Absolutely not

I don't want to play a game

While somebody else

Decides whether I get to live or die

Thank you very much

I need to think of a way out of here

Before they kill me first

ERIN: Well don't we all die eventually?

HUGH: That's rather fucking hippie dippie of you

Considering I'm tied to a chair

And my chances of being killed

Are significantly higher than yours right now

ERIN: Why are you here then?

HUGH: I don't know

I just remember being at the petrol station.

ERIN: Na.

Why are you here – here.

In X Land

Saib.

Who were you visiting?

HUGH: I came for a funeral/

ERIN: Who's funeral?

Saib.

ERIN: Who's funeral?

HUGH: It's none of your business

ERIN: Who's funeral?

HUGH: I'm finding your prying really quite intrusive

ERIN: Who's funeral?

Saib.

If you don't want to say

That's alright

Saib.

But

100

Where's your Dad Hugh?

Saib.

Hugh

Where's your Dad?

HUGH: It was his funeral.

ERIN: And was your Dad a

    Respectful

    Successful

    Good Father?

HUGH: What's my dead Dad got to do with this?

ERIN: Answer the question Hugh.

    She walks towards him looking at his arms.

ERIN: Wow

    You've got really hairy arms

HUGH: Of course they are

    I'm a grown fucking man

    ERIN pulls out some of HUGH's arm hairs.

HUGH: WHAT THE FUCK

ERIN: WOW

    That's loads!

    You going to answer the question now then Hugh?

    Was your Dad an honest man?

HUGH: I suppose so

    Yes.

ERIN: Odd?

HUGH: Odd.

ERIN presses play on a music device. Music plays extremely loudly. It needs to make everyone jump and go to cover their ears.

There is a movement sequence that shows ERIN is dancing along to it – ferociously, limbs flailing. In no way is this pretty. HUGH is trying his best to scream over the top of the music, but it is so loud it is impossible to hear him.

The lighting changes and we are now interweaved with a "flashback".

ERIN picking up the mind-maps that have been disbursed on the floor, that are also projected all over the AV. She's realised that who she has been waiting for has arrived a specific destination.

WOMAN: Thank you for contributing/

We've revised your details/
There is a 10% likelihood/
Because of how small the likelihood/
Process further/
Thank you for the concern/

News Reader: Today the country is grieving for our ex minister
He was a respectable, family man and we
as a nation are
going to miss him as
our leader very much.
I'm sure that, you, the
public agree we are
all indebted to him for
leading us to our glory.
We are sending the very
best of wishes to his son at
the funeral and celebration
of his life.

The lighting changes back and we snap back into present.

ERIN locks eyes with him, inching in closer. When it looks like she's about to kiss him, she stops the music.

DAU

She lifts his eye lids one at a time and about to shine a light on them, a poor attempt at being a doctor.

ERIN: They've asked me

   To check you for concussion

   How many fingers am I holding up?

HUGH: Five

ERIN: How many fingers am I holding up?

HUGH: Five

ERIN: How many fingers am I holding up?

HUGH: Ugh

   Pump, right?

ERIN: No

   Four and a thumb

HUGH: Four and a thumb

ERIN: See

   You can do it

   Well done you.

   What's the last thing you remember then?

HUGH: I was at a petrol station.

ERIN: You were at a petrol station.

HUGH: I was just putting the pump back down

ERIN: You were putting the pump back down

HUGH: When I

   Something,

   Hit

   My head/

ERIN: GREAT

   Well done you

   Sure you're fine

And you don't have concussion

Well,

Pretty sure

But

I'm so sorry Hugh

Because

It was me that hit you

Over the head

I know

A woman

Young

And small

Like me

Hitting you

Shock

Horror!

But it was and order

You fell to the floor

Right next to your car.

The boy behind the till was a great help to getting you
into the car

So I brought you here

I dragged you all the way over to there

And considering your size

It was a lot easier to get you in that chair than i
thought

But you're here now.

Pause. HUGH is staring at ERIN.

104

ERIN looks checking behind her after a moment.

ERIN: What are you looking at?

HUGH: You

You

Kidnapped me

ERIN: I'm so sorry

But

Yes

HUGH: Why –

Why me/

ERIN: I didn't have any choice

I had to

HUGH: I guess it

Explains why my head is pounding

And how I got this –

On my head.

You

Really

Hit

Me?

ERIN: Exactly.

But I'm going to help you

Promise

HUGH: Untie me then!

ERIN: I can't do that

(Not yet)

You have to play

Win your way out

That is the only way

ERIN picks up the rubix cube, mulling this over.

ERIN: Have you ever finished a rubix cube before?

HUGH: Na

I don't think so

ERIN: No, you don't look like you could either.

HUGH: Why/

ERIN: You look too –

You just don't look like the type

HUGH: What's that supposed to mean?!

Give us a go and I'll show you that I can

Ond

You'll have to untie –

Ugh

You'll –

You'll have to/

ERIN: Uncuff?

Unlock?

Untie?

HUGH: Why does it do that?

Make a simple word sound really complicated.

I don't know why you all still care so much

For a language that's completely irrelevant to the rest of us

ERIN: Look Hugh

I'm not going to

Uncuff

Unlock

or

Untie

You,

Not until the right moment

And maybe even then–

Not yet okay?

I need you to answer a couple of questions first.

And either you can do that

The easy,

collaborative way,

or

They'll make it difficult for you

They'll make sure

That they'll get the answer from you

Whichever way they can

Torture.

HUGH laughs – a disbelief.

ERIN: I'm not a liar.

HUGH laughs more.

ERIN: Don't laugh

I'm totally serious!

HUGH: Jesus Christ

Oh whoops

Sorry sorry sorry

Jesus Christ

This is just –

Well well

It's just that well

POPTY-FUCKING-PING

This is so ridiculous

I can't believe

That a little girl

Has tied me up

And

And is threatening me with torture

I can't take you seriously

AT ALL

ERIN: *(Kicking him in the groin.)* NOBODY SAYS POPTYPING

HUGH: FUCK
AH

ERIN: You think I'm lying?

HUGH: I don't/
What's celwee-ddog?

ERIN: Darllenwch y cyfiethiad

HUGH: Can't –
Can't really look up right now…

ERIN: If celwiddgi is "liar"
    Lying is…

    If you're a

    Liar

    Liar is the name for someone who lies.

    Lying is the verb

So –

HUGH: Lying.

ERIN: You catch on quite quickly really don't you

Which way will it be then Hugh?

ERIN goes to kick him again but is stopped.

HUGH: I'll answer!

I swear

I'll do anything

Please.

Just

Don't –

hurt me.

ERIN: Bit late for that.

HUGH: No please don't/

ERIN prods at the wound on his head and holds it. HUGH winces.

*Swell of Throbbing Gristle – We Hate You (Little Girls).
Lights change and take us to a flashback.*

*On the AV screen appears a woman, ERIN watches this
screen intently.*

WOMAN: Thank you for contributing your claim to the justice
system.

We've revised the details of your case and with the
support of our algorithm system, there is only a 10%
likelihood for the case reported.

Because of the sufficiently low likelihood of the case
taking place, it's highly unlikely that your case will be
processed any further.

Thank you for your concern and for taking the time to
keep your country safe.

We see ERIN break.

WOMAN: Thank you thank you thank

Thank you for contributing your case

We've revised

Details

details

dec-deci

decided that there's only a 10% 10%

10%

10%

10%

likelihood

Because of the sufficiently low likelihood

it's highly unlikely that your case will be processed any

further.

it's highly unlikely

it's highly unlikely

highly highly highly

your case will be processed any further

it's highly unlikely

unlikely

unlikely

Then with a very short movement sequence that is filled with the following dialogue

VOICE: REMEMBER: THE PARENTS ARE TO BLAME
HASHTAG SPOILER,
SHE KILLED HIM

BANISH

EXHILE

MURDERDER

ERIN: unlikely

TRI

We return to present day lighting. Like a dream, ERIN snaps out of the moment that haunts her. Mae'n dechrau bwrw glaw.
ERIN takes it in.

ERIN: I love the rain

Lots of people don't

They think it's an inconvenience

But I always have.

When I walking back from school

I used to just stop in it

Take my shoes off

And just run through it

Because you get soaked more if you run

And I'm not talking about some

Little April showers

No

I'm talking about the type

As though the heavens have opened

And the drops pound your skin

Sometimes leaving tiny bruises

So I would stop in the same place every time

Right on the top of the hill

And I would stand in it

Taking it all in

Just to make sure

That I could still feel

And it had soaked me right through

I loved the way that it smelled

Perfume of the rain.

You thirsty Hugh?

HUGH: I still have that vodka taste in my mouth.

ERIN: Are you thirsty?

HUGH: Yes.

She walks to her desk, to pull out a deck of cards and a panda pop, she finds a straw for it in amongst the clutter.

ERIN: This is how this game works

They're the ones asking the questions

You answer correctly

And you can have a drink.

Understand?

HUGH nods.

ERIN: And if you don't

Well/

Oh my god.

We should do it like The Chase.

Oh

Even better

Mastermind.

Ie.

Mastermind.

And I can be Magnus Magnusson.

Named as though his parents wanted him to be
bullied but/

HUGH: Are you enjoying this?

ERIN: Yes I am.

I really like games.

HUGH: So this is a game to you?

Everyone getting a kick

Out of the fact I'm being held

Like a fucking prisoner?

ERIN: Yes I am

To be totally honest with you.

She shuffles the cards and lays them out equally in three piles.

ERIN: You can choose which card

Pause.

Are you stupid or something?

Choose a fucking card!

HUGH: That one

ERIN: C'mon

Choose a pile

One

Two

or

Three

HUGH: That one –

One

Picking up a cards.

ERIN: Your full name is Hugh Jenkins?

HUGH: Ye.

She allows him a sip of the panda pop.

ERIN: Ta-da!

They stare at each other for a moment.

ERIN: Pick again.

HUGH: Ugh

Two

Picking up a cards.

ERIN: Were you born and bred here?

HUGH: Ye.

She allows him another sip of the panda pop.

ERIN: Ta-da!

He tries to drink a lot of it. ERIN pulls it away when she realises what he's doing.

She flicks him on the nose, a punishment.

ERIN: Don't cheat!

HUGH: Ah Jesus

My eyes are watering

C'mon!

ERIN: You have to earn it

Again

C'mon mun,

It's not hard

HUGH: Three

Picking up a cards.

ERIN: Was your father the leader of this country?

HUGH: Ye.

ERIN: Ta-da!

She allows him another sip of the panda pop, this time he plays by the rules.

ERIN: Again

HUGH: Two.

Picking up a cards.

ERIN: What about your mother?

HUGH: What/

ERIN: Your mother?

HUGH: How do you/

ERIN: She taught you the language?

HUGH: I can't

Please/

ERIN: What about your Mum, Hugh?

Pause.

If you don't answer my question Hugh,

They're going to make this a lot worse for you

Pause.

"MYFANWY" what was the last thing I searched?

MYF: Water Table.

Do you want to use

Water Table?

ERIN: Hugh

Do you know what Water Table –

No,

Water Table sounds crap.

Try again MYFANWY.

MYF: Water Cover?

ERIN: Water Cover?

Because it covers your face

No

Try again

MYF: Water Plank?

ERIN: No

Try again

MYF: Water Boarding

ERIN: Ye

Water Boarding

Do you know what "Water Boarding" is Hugh?

MYFANWY

Give Hugh a translation

MYF: Water Boarding

Or "Styllen Ddŵr",

Is a kind of torture

Where water is poured over a cloth

And placed over your face and breathing holes

In order to close the oxygen off just enough

To make the person feel like they're drowning.

Pause.

ERIN: Sound like something you'd like to experience Hugh?

HUGH: Not really, no

ERIN: Answer the question then

Please.

HUGH: I'm not really sure why

But you're very angry for such a little girl

Has anyone ever told you that?

ERIN walks to find a cloth and a case of panda pops.

HUGH: NO NO

Please

COME BACK

I was only joking

It was just a joke

Where are you going?

No I didn't mean it

Please –

ERIN goes to pour a bottle over the cloth, to dampen it.

ERIN: I'm sorry Hugh

But this is the procedure

If you don't co-operate / with them

HUGH: Please

Don't.

ERIN goes to hold the cloth on HUGH's face.

HUGH: Please!!

NO!

I'll tell you

She stops.

Please

ERIN pulls the cloth away from HUGHs face.

HUGH: I have reason to believe/

I think my Mother is dead.

ERIN: Believe?

HUGH: Yes.

I've not seen or heard from-

Well for a long time

And I don't –

I can't speak the language

Because it was for spending time with Mum

Our own secret code.

ERIN: So

How'd she go?

Pause.

ERIN put cloth on HUGH's face and pours from the bottle over the cloth.

HUGH: NO

I'll – I'll

Tell you.

Pause.

The last time I saw her,

Her and my Father were arguing.

My father always had a temper,

And he battered her-

Well all of us really

But she got the brunt of it, I think.

And one night,

They were rowing

I don't remember what about

I heard her screaming at him,

Proper screaming

Animal

Guttural

Screams.

It got worse somehow,

That bad that even a kid knows it's not right So

I got up out of bed,

And I walked downstairs

I peaked my head through the living room door

I could see her backed in to the corner

I walked in

I remember

Saying

"Mami – what's the matter?"

She said

"Nothing love, go back to bed"

And I remember her face being red and wet

My father then –

Slammed the door in my face.

And,

I

Believed her.

So I went back to bed.

The next thing

Thud against something solid

Crac

And the screaming stopped

I never –

Saw her again

I tried asking

My father

But I never got anything from him.

Quiet

Every time

No matter how much I tried,

Nothing.

So after years,

Of asking,

I stopped,

Asking.

And I couldn't bring myself to –

Speak the language.

ERIN: But you're speaking it now with me.

HUGH: Ye cos you're making me

ERIN: Making you.

HUGH: Oh whatever!

Too many people are so fucking precious

Your language isn't perfect anyway

If your biggest problem

Is preserving its purity

You need to open your fucking eyes

And roll with the times

ERIN: Without purists

Like me

Like my family

We'd still be slaves

To them

Over the bridge

You understand that?

Without extremists

Radicalism

The blood and guts

For change

We would still believe

That, that was all we deserved

Easy for you

I'm sure

Getting to run away

And forget who you are –

COME ON

Pick!

HUGH: Three

Picking up a card.

ERIN: Did you fail Law School?

HUGH: How do you...

Nobody knows –

ERIN: They have ways

Of finding out what we need

HUGH: What do they want with me?

  I'm tied up,

  Speaking your language

  Playing some fucking card game

  Do they want money?

  If you let me go I can get you/

ERIN: They don't want money

  I just want you to answer my questions

Pick a pile

HUGH: One

  Picking up a card.

ERIN: Do you have any brothers or sisters?

HUGH: No

  Two

Picking up a card.

ERIN: Why don't you live here anymore?

HUGH: I got

  Sent away

  After finishing school

  My Father

  Wanted me to go and learn about myself.

ERIN: And did you?

HUGH: I suppose I did

  Ye

ERIN: What did you learn?

  Pause.

  What did you learn?

HUGH: I don't know

I can't really think right now

ERIN: What did you learn?

HUGH: I don't really remember

I'm a bit tied up.

ERIN: What did you learn?

HUGH: Why do you care?

No, seriously

Why do you want to know?

It's not like –

I don't see

Any sort of microphone or-

Or hear

For that matter

Any sort of feed

Telling you what to ask

ERIN: What do you mean?

HUGH: You haven't even –

Left this room once

You haven't even received any sort of call

ERIN: No

But I got a call

From God

HUGH: There's –

There's not even anything written on those cards

Oh for fuck sake

Fuck

HUGH starts to laugh.

It's –

YOU

Isn't it?!

ALL OF THIS?!

ERIN: Ah shit

Good guess!

HUGH: ARE YOU FUCKING SERIOUS

How could I be so fucking stupid

None of this is real

There isn't a "they" is there?

You're just a fucking psycho little bitch

It's all you

Isn't it?

ISN'T IT?

UNTIE ME

NOW

OR I SWEAR/

ERIN: I'm awfully sorry

But I can't do that

HUGH: Why?!

ERIN: Because you're a little angry right now

HUGH: Because you're holding me as a fucking prisoner!

Or are you enjoying using me

Like a puppet or something?

Am I bait?

For something

Or someone else?

You dragged me back to

What?

Your little Wendy house?

Your bunker?

You think this is all some sort of game?

I'm so confused

I just want to go home

Please

Let me go home

I have a family

And they need me

Please

I don't

I don't

WHY

I don't deserve this

I bet

Ye

I bet you're just some sick

Stalker

Domineering bitch

That gets off from cuffing people up.

ERIN: That would be fun I'm sure

But no

That's not my style

HUGH: Then why am I –

Why me?

ERIN: Because I've been waiting

For you.

Is that what you wanted to hear?

HUGH: You've been waiting/

ERIN: Yes

Waiting

That's what I said

Another card then.

Saib. ERIN grabs a steel hook that is hanging from the ceiling, looks at it, holds the sharp end and hits him with the handle on the funny bone with it.

HUGH: AH!

ERIN: Come on then

HUGH: How can I when you keep hurting me?

ERIN: Pick another card and maybe I'll stop hurting you.

HU GH: I DON'T WANT TO PLAY I

WANT TO GO HOME

ERIN: Having a strop are we?

HUGH: You're changing the rules to suit you

ERIN: Of course I'm changing the rules

To suit me

It's my game

I can do whatever I want

She licks his face, he tries to wipe his own face but his hands are still tied to the chair.

HUGH: UGH

That's

That's

Disgusting

HOW DARE YOU

HOW DARE YOU LICK ME

Like a

Like a

Fucking

DOG

Like a fucking bitch

ERIN: Ye.

She puts the meat hook back in its place.

Now pick a card

Unless you want me to lick the other side too

HUGH: Get-get your fucking spit off my face

The way it's drying on my face

It's fucking gross

ERIN: You don't want more?

Pick then.

HUGH: Three.

She picks up another card.

ERIN: Oh.

Here's an interactive question.

ERIN presses play on a tape, it plays the following dialogue.

VOICE 1: Hello?

HUGH'S VOICE: Hello.

VOICE 1: Helloooooooooooo

HUGH: Hello!

VOICE 1: Are you there?

HUGH'S VOICE: Yes I'm here! Are you?

VOICE 1: I'm waiting.

HUGH'S VOICE: Tell me where and I'll come and find you.

VOICE 1: Hello?

HUGH'S VOICE: Yes I'm here!!

VOICE 1: Helloooooooooooo

ERIN stops the tape.

Saib.

ERIN: Familiar?

HUGH: *(Shrugs.)* No

She presses play.

VOICE 1: Hello?

HUGH'S VOICE: : I told you, I'm here!!

VOICE 1: Helloooooooooooo HUGH'S

VOICE: I've been waiting for ages

ERIN stops the tape.

ERIN: Now?

HUGH: I've never heard that before.

ERIN doesn't believe him.

Hugh: What?

I haven't!

It's fucking weird/

She presses play.

VOICE 1: Hello?

HUGH'S VOICE: I've been really looking forward to this

VOICE 1: Hellooooooooooooo

ERIN stops the tape.

HUGH: Honestly.

I don't know what that is.

I don't know –

I don't know who those voices belong to

But/

ERIN: Liar

HUGH: It wasn't me

That's not me.

ERIN: And what is "that" then?

You're pretty sure that it WASN'T you

So do tell,

What is it that you think you didn't do?

Pause.

HUGH: I didn't understand a word of that. ERIN:

Read the fucking translation then

What is it that you think that you didn't do?

HUGH: Don't know

It's not me

I didn't/

ERIN presses play on the tape again. The tapes dialogue continues.

HUGH'S VOICE: C'mon stop being such a tease.

VOICE 1: Are you there?

ERIN: Is that your voice on
the tape?

Is that your voice on the tape?Is
that your voice on the tape?*ERIN*

pokes HUGH in the eye.

HUGH: AH FUCK

I'm playing your stupid
fucking game

ERIN: Is that your voice on
the tape?

Pause.

HUGH: NO MORE

I CAN'T/

Please.

Don't make me listen to it back.

ERIN: Do you want to be
completely blind Hugh?

Is that your voice on the tape?

ERIN grabs HUGH's face and goes to poke the other eye.

HUGH: Yes!

*ERIN stops the tape. Still playing by her rules she takes her time
removing herself and allows him another sip of the panda pop.*

ERIN: Who are you talking with?

HUGH: Don't know their real name.

Just –

ERIN: What?

HUGH: Ugh sounds stupid.

HUGH'S VOICE: I can't wait to
see you

VOICE 1 Hello?

HUGH'S VOICE:Ugh don't
start that again

VOICE 1: Hellooooooooooooo

HUGH'S VOICE: Please don't
make me beg for it

VOICE 1: Are you there?

HUGH'S VOICE:You know I
want you

VOICE 1: Hello?

ERIN: Just say it.

HUGH: I only know –

Their username.

ERIN: Which is?

I'm sure I've got a spoon in the draw somewhere

Could just use it to pull one of your eyes out? It's easy
enough

Crows do it to lambs all the time

Just for a bit of fun.

Not with a spoon of course

But I'm sure I could manage/

HUGH: Faze.

She allows him another sip of the panda pop.

ERIN sits back down in her chair.

ERIN: Do you have any idea why you're here with me now
Hugh?

HUGH: No.

ERIN: Think now
Before shouting out

You can have a clue.

*ERIN dials a number into her remote, the screen displays a phone
call being made. ERIN walks HUGH and, take the ringing phone out of
his pocket and holds it up. It displays the name "FAZE" as an
incoming call.*

She leaves it to ring out, leaving an answer phone message. ERIN

ERIN AS VOICE 1: Hello?

HUGH: What the – ?

ERIN as VOICE 1: Helloooooooooooooo

HUGH: Fuck

But you can't be Faze/

She hangs up the phone.

ERIN: Erin will do nicely, thanks.

HUGH: What kind of sick person are you?

ERIN: I was going to ask you the same question.

HUGH: So all those chats were you the whole time?

ERIN: You catch on quick Hugh.

HUGH: *(Gagging.)* I – I'm gonna/

ERIN: If you could try not to, that would be great

Because it smells so much

And it'll make me throw up too

And there will be such a mess

And I don't really want to waste time cleaning

Because I've put so much effort in already

To get you here Hugh.

HUGH: Are you some sort of glory hunter?

A venus fly trap?

Well you've fucked it already love

Couldn't be a worse vigilante even if you tried

Becasue if I go down

You're fucking coming with me

Think what they'll do to you

Kidnapping son of the Minister

ERIN: The thing is Hugh

I don't care about that Hugh

I don't care at all what they'll do to me Hugh

Because we all have to go in the end Hugh

And I might as well go over something worth fighting for

Hugh

Hugh

H-u-g-h

Who's idea was it to spell it with silent letters?

HUGH: I dunno

Just always spelt it that way

ERIN: Well you're spelling it wrong

Huw

Every

Colour

HUGH: Hugh every colour?

It sounded like an insult when it came out of your mouth

But I'm not sure that it is.

ERIN: Joke a minute are you Hugh?

ERIN removes HUGH's shoes and socks. I'll

make you laugh now

HUGH: What are you doing?

What the fuck are you doing?!

Get off me!

Get off me!

Don't you-

Don't you fucking touch me

ERIN starts to tickle his feet.

What?

Are you actually tickling me?

Is this a joke?

Or all part of your little dominatrix bitch act?

ERIN still tickling his feet for an uncomfortable amount of time.

HUGH: The thing is Erin

I'm not into Knismolagnia

Because I'm actually not ticklish

At all

Anywhere

Never have been

ERIN: Fuck.

HUGH: You aren't capable of this

I know you aren't

I can see it in you

You're too nice

Too weak

To go through with anything like this

This isn't you

I know you're type

ERIN: You don't know the first thing about me

ERIN presses play on the tapes again, they play on loop and they get louder each time it louder.

I am Faze

I'm the one you've been speaking to all night

I'm the one you've been asking for pictures from

I'm the one you were so
eager to meet.

HUGH:
Please
I don't!
I never really –
I'm not what you think –
I'll answer more questions
I swear.

ERIN turns them off.

ERIN: Choose a card then.

HUGH: One

ERIN: Where were you on the 20th of November, two years
ago?

Pause.

HUGH: I dunno.

ERIN: Don't you?

HUGH: No

I don't

Why would I?

I don't –

I ugh –

I don't remember.

ERIN: I'm going to ask you again Hugh.

Give you the 'benefit of the doubt'

Like they say.

Where were you on the 20th of November, two years ago?

HUGH: I've said,

I don't remember!

ERIN: Are you lying

    Because you think I don't know already?

    The whole point of the game

    Is that you confess

HUGH: Confess?

You're confused.

I haven't anything to/

ERIN: No bullshit Hugh

    Or would you like that bright light back on

    That you loved so much

HUGH: What do you want me to confess?

    I've never been charged

So in the eyes of the law –

ERIN: But the two of us

    Know differently

    And just because the fucking algorithms

    Think that you haven't done anything

    We know the truth

    Don't we?

HUGH: Whatever you think I've done

    You're wrong It's a

    guaranteed

    Faultless system/

ERIN: Faultless system

    For you, maybe.

    If you have something to hide

Well,

You're right

A totally faultless system.

HUGH: I don't

Nothing to hide.

ERIN: Where is Gethin then?

Pause. ERIN stares HUGH dead in the eye. HUGH – the penny has finally dropped.

HUGH: What?

ERIN: Come on Hugh

What have you got to lose?

You can confide in me.

Pause.

ERIN: Three years ago *(Storm outside gets progressively worse.)*

Fragger started talking online with Destroyer

They became very close

Very quickly/

Destroyer said to Fragger

That he understood exactly what it was like to be alone,

No friends,

A dad that hurts everyone

All this bullshit

And started some kind of –

Destroyer persuaded Fragger

To meet

To play

The evening of the 20th of November

Expecting to meet another boy

But who turned up?

You.

A man

Nearly in his thirties

A man who'd been Grooming

My son/

HUGH: Your son?

ERIN: Yes – my son!

And I want to know every tiny detail

From the day he left

How

When

And why

Tell me!

HUGH avoids eye contact.

Or did you hit a seven-year-old boy

Over the head

And carry him off too?

I've been waiting

Lying awake

Standing in the shit

Suffocating

For two years now

For a tangible answer

If my son is still alive

And I've never been one

To keep quiet or polite

So I decided to do something

Because there's nothing else for me to lose

My son has disappeared

And the only thing I had left,

Were the conversations you had

Saved on his computer.

You took everything from me.

And here you are now

In a fucking abattoir with me.

So tell me

Just say

Where is Gethin?

Pause.

Where is Gethin?

Where is Gethin?

Where is Gethin?

Hugh

Where is Gethin?

Where is Gethin?

Where is Gethin?

She grabs his thumb with the intent to break it.

Where is Gethin?

HUGH: AH/

A sudden high pitched ringing, ERIN fumbles to the ground.

ERIN: no no no no no no no no

DISTORTED VOICE: I'm sorry to interrupt but I have

an emergency

I'm sorry to interrupt

My child

My child/

ERIN: GETHIN/

DISTROTEDVOICE: I'm sorry to interrupt but I have an emergency, my child has gone missing

The ringing stops. ERIN takes a deep breath, she knows she can't succumb to that moment, she has a job to do now.

ERIN: You thirsty?

You look thirsty

Do you want another drink?

DRINK

NOW

She forces the panda pop and straw into his mouth.

He gulps.

He tries to stop but ERIN isn't moving it away like before.

She wants him to drink it all.

You see

There is one thing

As a parent

That I hate myself for in this situation,

And I go over and over

Every second

Trying to figure it out

The whole situation

How could I have taught him

140

To never trust strangers

And every time

It comes back to the fact that you are an adult

And you should know better

Because you've just finished

A concoction of a panda pop

And a shit load of Fentanyl

And what you're experiencing now

Is pharmaceutical torture

Which is

The use of drugs

To punish

Or

To draw

Information out of a person.

So if you want to live

Hugh

You better co-operate

And answer my fucking question

WHERE

IS

GETHIN?

Pause.

HUGH's consciousness begins to waver.

This is echoed with a distortion of the storm outside.

HUGH: Even if you do kill me

Even if you do

You

You can't

Stop

This

This

The cycle.

The algo

Fucking

Rhythyms

The circle

They've got him.

Because

There's more

And they're–

Especially…

HUGH realises what he was about to say.

The rain gets heavier, there's a low rumble of thunder in the distance.

ERIN: What?

Especially what?

Pause.

Especially fucking what?

Especially fucking WHAT Hugh?!

HUGH: THEM

        The circle/

ERIN: What's the circle/

HUGH groans.

ERIN: WHERE IS GETHIN?

PLEASE

I don't want to kill you

I just want Gethin back

It's your turn to do the right thing Hugh

Here's your chance

To be a good person

Are you going to take it?

Pause – HUGH is practically unconscious from the sedative to make any sense.

ERIN: Fuck sake Hugh

She smacks him.

Wake up!

ERIN: FOR FUCK SAKE!

Flood of music

ERIN'S VOICE: He still hasn't come back.

MAN'S VOICE: I've told you, our team's on their way to do an
inspection.

ERIN'S VOICE: You don't understand, he was supposed to be
home hours ago.

MAN'S VOICE: I'm sure he's still out playing. Have you checked
every relationship he has? What about his dad?

ERIN'S VOICE: No! He's never been in the picture. There's
something wrong and you're not listening to me!

MAN'S VOICE: I'm sorry Ms but you have to calm down,
there's no need to shout, you're getting hysterical. This is
procedure.

ERIN'S VOICE: It's not! There's something wrong, I just know.

MAN'S VOICE: I'm sure everything is fine. Most of the time
they've just run off somewhere, we'll find him.

ERIN'S VOICE: Why aren't you listening to me?

MAN'S VOICE: I am, but he's a young lad. I remember when I was his age...

ERIN'S VOICE: Call it mother's instinct. But there's something fucking wrong!

WOMAN: It's extremely unlikely that your report will be processed any further.

It's extremely unlikely that your report will be processed any further.

It's extremely unlikely that your report will be processed any further.

It's extremely unlikely that your report will be processed any further.

It's extremely unlikely that your report will be processed any further.

ERIN shakes her head.

ERIN: You have to still be here.

WOMAN: Thank you for your concern and for taking the time to keep your country safe.

PEDWAR

An hour or two later like we've pressed fast forward slightly on a remote control.

ERIN sits in front of him eating beans from a baked bean tin.

ERIN: C'mon

She gets up to look at his breathing.

Fucking wake up

Fucking prick.

She stares at him.

She flicks his nose, hard.

HUGH gives a low tired groan.

ERIN: Welcome back

Did you have a nice nap?

He can barely open his eyes or hold his head up, another low groan.

ERIN: You back with us alright?

Can you speak?

Hugh? HUGH!

HUGH grunts. Unable to really comprehend.

ERIN: Can you open your eyes?

She gives an exhale – perhaps pity.

Do you need some sugar?

Maybe I've got a Milky-way somewhere.

She goes back to the mess she's created. In amongst it, she finds a fun size Milky-way.

She unwraps it.

ERIN: Take some

He can't actively take any. She breaks the

top half of the chocolate off.

ERIN: You have to suck on it

Don't bite

She places the tiny slab of chocolate in his mouth.

With her finger near his mouth, HUGH attempts to bite her, but just misses.

ERIN: Fucking bastard

Did you just try and bite me?

HUGH doesn't respond.

ERIN: Did you just try and fucking bite me?

You some dog that bites people are you?

Do you know what we do

With dogs that fucking bite people

On the farm?

HUGH spits in her face.

ERIN: *(Wiping it off calmly.)* Do you think a bit of spit

Is going to put me off?

After so long?

After how far?

A little too late for that

Don't you think?

We're

'in too deep'

Like they say.

ERIN eats the fun sized milky bar.

Pause.

HUGH: Why didn't you kill me when you had the chance?

ERIN: There was a moment where I thought about it

But

In the end

Death is too good for you

In death you can start again

And if I have to carry on

Crawling through this shit every day

146

Then certainly,

You don't get to leave,

You don't get to forget who you are

I'd much rather

That you suffer with me.

HUGH: You make it sound like

I should say

Thank you/

Or be

Grateful

Fucking grateful for only

Kidnapping me

Tying me up

Pulling my arm hairs out

Water boarding me

Kicking me in the bollocks

Trying to tickle me

Poking me in the eye

And

Drugging me

OH

Thank you so fucking much

ERIN: A little ungrateful,

If you ask me

I could have just killed you straight away

HUGH: Do it then!

Not a day passes

Where I don't think about letting the river

Just fucking swallow me anyway

ERIN: You think you're the only one?

You think you're the only one who suffers?

You must realise

That everything you do

Has an effect

It effects people

People's lives

People's hearts

People's families

HUGH: Maybe you're right

I dunno

Maybe I just don't understand it

Maybe I just can't

Comprehend –

Pause.

Ugh

I've always known I was

That I wanted/

Ugh

I dunno

Maybe

I was

Bored.

And it was easy

It was easy to persuade

That it's just what 'friends' did.

The two of them sit in this information.

ERIN: You started

    Because you were

    Bored?

HUGH: I think

    Ye –

Maybe.

ERIN: I don't believe you.

    If you were bored

    You should have got a fucking hobby.

HUGH: Erin,

    I know it's awful

    And I can't undo what I've done

    But I can help you now

    Think

    If you let me go…

    Now

    I could

    Actually

    Help you.

ERIN: You've helped enough.

HUGH: I'm sorry Erin

    Is that what you want to hear?

    Is that what you need

    To let me go?

ERIN: NO

YOU DON'T UNDERSTAND

I don't want your apology

I want to know where Gethin is

HUGH: There is a chance/

ERIN: Fuck

HUGH: I'll tell you/

ERIN: Where is he?

HUGH: If you untie me.

Maybe it'll all come flooding back.

ERIN: Bullshit

HUGH: Fine

Have it your way.

But trust me

I won't say anything else

Until you let me go

ERIN: I'm not unreasonable.

You promise,

On your family's life –

And tell me everything

And I mean fucking everything

You know

About Gethin,

His whereabouts –

And I'll let you go.

HUGH: Promise.

ERIN: Say it then.

Formally

In the

Legal way

C'mon promise,

With the whole truth and nothing but the truth,

Now!

HUGH: I swear in the name of God that what I shall state shall be the truth, the whole truth and nothing but the truth.

Pause.

ERIN standing directly in front of his face, reminding him of the task in hand.

HUGH: It is most likely that they have moved Gethin moved on.

ERIN: He's still alive?

HUGH: As far as I'm aware

Yes.

ERIN: I KNEW IT

I never stopped thinking

That he was still alive.

Where is he?

HUGH: I don't know.

ERIN: You don't know?

How do you not know?

HUGH: YOU SAID YOU'D UNTIE ME

ERIN: Untie you for it's 'most likely'?

I don't think so/

HUGH: YOU SAID

YOU CAN'T LIE ERIN

YOU SAID

AND I DELIVERED

DON'T BE A LIAR

You said

You're not playing fair/

ERIN: Don't you talk to me about what's fair

Why don't you know?!

HUGH: I had to give Gethin up

Erin

I know how it sounds

But I had to pay the price

To ensure

Subtlety and silence

But I had to

I didn't have any other choice

I had to protect my own

You've no idea how difficult a decision it was

Having to –

Having to give him up

Erin

The two of us are looking for him/

ERIN: You're seriously trying it aren't you

How fucking dare you

We're not both looking for him together

We're not a team

You're disgusting

And you've ruined my life

I'm not going to untie you for

152

"it's most likely"

That's fucking bullshit

I'm going to fucking kill you

Why don't you know?

Where is he?

You're the one who lured,

Groomed/

HUGH: LOVED/

ERIN: DON'T YOU FUCKING DARE/

HUGH: When they took him from me/

ERIN grabs him by the scruff then grabs his face, trying to suffocate him, but not very well.

ERIN: I don't want to hear it

I don't want to hear your pity party

I am his mother

And I know he wouldn't have gone willingly with you,

I know my son

You stole him

You stole my child

You stole a child from his mother

From his home

Ripped him from me when my back was turned

And when he didn't come back,

Fucking hell on earth began

And my womb screams for him every fucking second

Because he is a part of me

He's my every single thought

And he is all that I have

And I will shout and scream until I know that he's safe

Back home

Where he's supposed to be

That is love.

Now tell me where the fuck he is

Now

Or I swear to God I'll/

She breaks and collapses into his lap.

I should rip your fucking tongue out.

We sit in this moment while HUGH regains his breath, it is not to be rushed.

HUGH: Erin

I'm sorry.

But you have to know

This

It's much bigger

Their control

It's much bigger than me.

They took him from me.

ERIN: "They"?

"The Circle"

You said

"You can't stop the cycle."

You said

"There's more"

Who did you mean?

HUGH: Erin/

ERIN: Who are they?

HUGH: Shut up and I'll tell you

But

You have to

Promise

You'll let me go

And I'll just

Disappear

ERIN picks up the rubix cube, continues it while she's thinking about this deal.

She's completed it, puts it back on the table.

ERIN sighs.

ERIN: Fine

Tell me

HUGH: These bots.

The algorithms.

They're propaganda

To make you believe it's for convenience.

They've been programmed,

Ensuring protection for this "select" group

And this group is growing

On every level

There are more and more people getting in on it

Police

Judges

Politicians

Everyone helping each other out

You scratch my back,

And we'll help you seek out the vulnerable.

Meetings

Sex parties

Burning down the buildings afterwards

Destroying the evidence

You name it

They'll help you

If the price is right.

Generally it's pictures,

But it has to be ones they've never seen before.

Or if it's riskier

Something of equivalent value.

And if some one

Or something

Slips through the net

Maybe someone finds the strength

To finally come forward

They are miraculously found dead before they get to
testify

These algorithms are put in place

To keep us,

Them

All of us

In place

All the circles are connected

It's rife Erin

And I'm just a fucking pawn,

Son of The First Minister,

Under the thumb,

I'm/

Nothing.

And they make that really fucking clear

They won't even give a shit that you've killed me.

If they knew you had me tied up

They'd just delete our entire existence

In the click of a finger

Because it's much much bigger Erin

A lot bigger than just tying me to a fucking chair

Pause.

ERIN: Is this the truth?

Why should I believe you?

HUGH: Dunno

I suppose you don't have to

But what else have you got

To get you closer to Gethin?

ERIN: Fucking

All of them

Making themselves comfortable.

HUGH: Ye.

The second someone gets brave

They'll defended them

"Oh no they couldn't possibly

They aren't that kind of person

They're far too nice

They contribute so much to our society

They couldn't possibly"

But it's lies of course

To protect each other.

It doesn't matter how well you paint yourself to others,

Everybody is capable of darkness

ERIN: And you –

You're disgusting.

But I'm going to hunt every single one of you

Pause. ERIN starts preparing to leave, she picks up HUGH's wallet from the desk.

HUGH: WAIT

Where are you going?

You said you'd let me go!

You can just leave me here

ERIN: That's exactly what I'm going to do

Because I want you to suffer

Slowly

And painfully

So I'm going to leave you to rot

I'm going to make you understand what it's like-

HUGH: What the fuck do you mean?

ERIN: Well

There is one thing

Actually

That I don't understand

But let's go back a little bit

For some context

Shall we?

You've got your own little girl

How can you exist

And do the things you do To

your own blood?

HUGH: No she's my daughter

Of course not

ERIN: So it's only other peoples children then.

HUGH: I know how it sounds –

ERIN: Are you a great Dad then Hugh?

Pause.

You can think about it if you want

Over and over

Cherish the memories

Imagine them

Because we're about to come

To some sort of bargain

Child for a child

She opens it up and holds a picture.

You've been helping them

Contributing to their cause

And now

You're going to pay for it

I'll pay for Gethin

Through infiltrating from inside the circle It's

the only way

So I'll pay the toll

With Mable

Revealing the picture she's hold is of Mable.

HUGH: Na

Erin

Leave her alone

ERIN: She's a pretty little thing isn't she

HUGH: Leave her out of this

ERIN: To late for that

Auntie Erin will pick her up from school

From Mrs Andrews' classroom/

HUGH: HOW DO YOU KNOW THAT/

ERIN: And we'll go for a little trip

And stop for tea at McDonald's/

HUGH: Don't you dare!/

ERIN: Because she loves their toys

Doesn't she?/

HUGH: Like the fuck am I going to tell you/

ERIN: And she can eat her chicken Mc-Nuggets

While we're on our way/

HUGH: Very fucking funny Erin,

You've had your joke now/

ERIN: To find the circle/

HUGH: NA

ERIN DON'T

IT WON'T WORK

THEY'LL KILL YOU

AND TAKE HER NO

HESITATION/

ERIN: It's over Hugh

There's nothing else you can say

I'm going to leave you to rot here

And while you rot

Think on the fact

That a person like you

Doesn't deserve the pleasure

Of the purest love from a child

You don't deserve the pleasure

The depth of a never ending and infinite love

There is no other feeling that even comes close to it

HUGH: SHUT THE FUCK UP

WHO THE FUCK ARE YOU TO DECIDE!

IF YOU TOUCH MY GIRL I'LL

I'LL FUCKING/

ERIN: Fucking what Hugh?

You're tied up

HUGH: Don't test me Erin

I'll fucking kill you

STAY AWAY FROM HER

ERIN: The thing is Hugh

You're dangerous

You've said it yourself

And I can't let someone Who's

a threat to society Back out, free

That would be irresponsible.

HUGH: You can't do this

   YOU CAN'T TAKE MABLE

You're fucking mental

ERIN: Yes I am "fucking mental"

   Do you understand now?

   Now that there's a threat

   Maybe you'll lose the person

   You love the most in the whole world

   Maybe now

   In this second

   You're beginning to understand

   The effect

   Of what you've really done

HUGH: NO

   YOU BITCH

   NO

   YOU CAN'T TAKE HER

   YOU CAN'T

   I WON'T LET YOU

   I WON'T FUCKING LET YOU

ERIN turns to leave, knowing what she has to do. HUGH snaps one end of the handcuffs and launches at ERIN, holds her in a choke from behind.

HUGH: I should fucking kill you.

> *There's a low grumble of thunder. We hear sirens. ERIN starts to grapple, trying to wriggle free.*

HUGH: What?

You really thought,

A little girl like you

There wouldn't be any consequences

I can't just let you get away with this

Sirens getting closer.

Oh – particularly because they are right outside.

Because when they see that you've kidnapped Me

(We know

They won't believe

Anything you say Erin)

And I'll say

It was self defence

The door is continuously being banged on.

POLICE V/O: Police, open up!

> *ERIN kicks/wriggles free she grabs the All in One Castration device and hits him over the head – knocking him sensless. The storm rages underscored*

The following happens along side the V/O.	*simultaneously* ERIN V/O: Not a second passes
This following sequence is stylised.	Where I don't listen to the whispers
	The poison in my mind
ERIN pulls the trousers and pants off of HUGH badly (In a way that is suggestive to	The pit in my stomach
	That says,

163

the audience, it is NOT vital
that we see nudity.)
She leans in and we hear a pop
and HUGH screams
She's castrated him
She picks up his bollocks

POLICE V/O: Open the door!

Open up now! *Etc.*

The sound of a door being bust open.

CHILD V/O: Mami?

ERIN turns, holding HUGH's balls, covered in blood.

ERIN: Fuck

You're still here

Because I don't have a choice

I have to find you and bring you back home

And when you're back I'll embrace you with every inch of my being

And love you for eternity.

SNAP BLACKOUT

WWW.OBERONBOOKS.COM

Follow us on Twitter @oberonbooks
& Facebook @OberonBooksLondon